PUB STROLLS IN

WARWICKSHIRE

Richard Shurey

COUNTRYSIDE BOOKS
NEWBURY BERKSHIRE

COUNTRYSIDE BOOKS
3 Catherine Road
Newbury, Berkshire

To view our complete range of books,
please visit us at
www.countrysidebooks.co.uk

ISBN 1 85306 674 5

Photographs by the author
Maps by the author and redrawn by
Gelder design & mapping

Designed by Graham Whiteman

Produced through MRM Associates Ltd., Reading
Printed by Woolnough Bookbinding Ltd., Irthlingborough

Contents

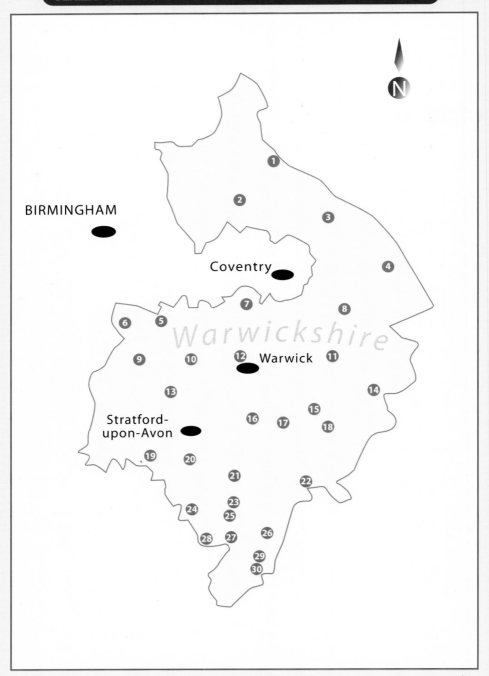

PUBLISHER'S NOTE

We hope that you obtain considerable enjoyment from this book; great care has been taken in its preparation. However, changes of landlord and actual closures are sadly not uncommon. Likewise, although at the time of publication all routes followed public rights of way or permitted paths, diversion orders can be made and permissions withdrawn.

We cannot, of course, be held responsible for such diversion orders and any inaccuracies in the text which result from these or any other changes to the routes nor any damage which might result from walkers trespassing on private property. We are anxious though that all details covering the walks and the pubs are kept up to date and would therefore welcome information from readers which would be relevant to future editions.

The sketch maps accompanying each walk are not always to scale and are intended to guide you to the starting point and give a simple but accurate idea of the route to be taken. For those who like the benefit of detailed maps, we recommend that you arm yourself with the relevant Ordnance Survey map in the Landranger series.

Oxford Dictionary: 'Stroll' – saunter or go for a short, leisurely walk. How apt then for the title of this series. These are not marathon hikes over vast distances. They are gentle ambles through the lovely Warwickshire countryside – and starting and/or finishing your excursion with refreshment at a traditional English pub, what could be nicer?

The pubs in Warwickshire are alive and surviving in spite of some talk about their demise. Publicans today have to try even harder to attract customers and this is reflected in the food and drink offered and the comfort of the surroundings. You are less likely to see that country character sitting smoking his pipe in the corner and observing and putting the world to rights. You are more guaranteed to find a pub where the welcome is warm – with more warmth coming from the blazing log fire in the inglenook in the winter months.

Warwickshire is a wonderfully varied landscape and we are unaware that the vast conurbations of Birmingham and Coventry nudge the county boundaries. The northern countryside was so vividly described by George Eliot in her books such as *Adam Bede*, *The Mill on the Floss* and *Middlemarch* – the countryside where villages 'lay in the central plain of what we are pleased to call Merry England'.

The south has the characteristics of a Cotswold limestone terrain with honey-hued cottages, stone walls and towns and villages that made fortunes from sheep in past days.

In the middle of the county is the land of Shakespeare where there are still pockets of woodland of the ancient Forest of Arden. Perhaps you will finish a walk here singing like the character in *As You Like It*, 'This life is most jolly'!

All this beautiful and so varied area is waiting to be discovered and the best way to get into the heart of the countryside is on foot. The rambles described take us to high hills that reach over 800 feet; there are strolls through mixed woodlands especially lovely in spring and autumn. Sometimes we are by the rivers such as the Avon and the Stour.

There are several canals in Warwickshire built over 200 years ago that are veritable arteries to often lonely but attractive rural places. Full use is made of towpaths on these strolls, especially as the bargees (like ramblers) needed refreshment – waterside pubs are often sited most conveniently!

All the rambles described in this book are suitable for family walks. Unfortunately many children today eschew using their feet wherever possible but I think they will all find something to interest them. The dog at least will always be enthusiastic. My loveable Meg was given a welcome at many pubs and if not allowed indoors could enjoy the pretty gardens.

Almost all the pubs have a car park for customers' use but it is only polite to obtain permission if you are leaving your vehicle while you walk.

So forget the problems and stress of this modern life; on with the boots, pop this book in your rucksack and follow in my footsteps to sample the many delights of Shakespeare's county by simple, leisurely strolls – delights for which the English living far abroad wistfully sigh.

Richard Shurey

Hartshill

The Anchor Inn

MAP: OS LANDRANGER 140 (GR 335946)	WALK 1	DISTANCE: 4 MILES

DIRECTIONS TO START: HARTSHILL IS 2 MILES NORTH-WEST OF NUNEATON. THE ANCHOR INN IS ON THE B4111 BY THE CANAL BRIDGE. **PARKING:** IN THE LARGE CAR PARK BY THE PUB.

The stroll is through an area which was devastated by industrialisation but is now being skilfully restored to delightful countryside; the old mine slag heaps are being regenerated with plant life. To add to the attractiveness of the walk there are two lovely features – the delightful Coventry Canal and the verdant square mile of the Hartshill Country Park.

The canal is 38 miles long and was completed in 1790; with a trade concentrating on the local coal it was a very successful waterway. The climb up to the park affords splendid views far over the Trent Valley; there is an information hut and café by the car park.

The little green at Hartshill has an unusual memory of the Warwickshire poet Michael Drayton who was born in the village in 1563 – the castle-like bus shelter was declared open by John Betjeman.

The Anchor Inn

This is a finely sited Everards pub for everyone, but for families it is a real treat as the children's playground is one of the best I have seen in any pub. Oh, if only I was young again! For the not so energetic there is the waterside garden where you can sit and watch the world (and the boats) go by. This was a favourite hostelry for the bargees although perhaps as a warning to modern sailors there is a bold notice of the Coventry Court case of 1861 when fines were imposed for the evasion of tolls! If it is not outside weather the pub has cosy bars with open inglenook fires – get Fido to ask if he can come in and the reply could well be favourable in this friendly pub.

The menu has plenty of good old-fashioned steaks but the Pork Ginger is a favourite of mine; the diet conscious can take their pick from the range of salad dishes; there is a selection of half a dozen vegetarian dishes and Monty's Menu of sizzling chips with everything is great for the youngsters. The Everards real ales are complemented by 'guests' such as Old Speckled Hen. The hours are 11.30 am to 3 pm and 5.30 pm to 11 pm with the normal Sunday hours. Telephone: 024 76398839.

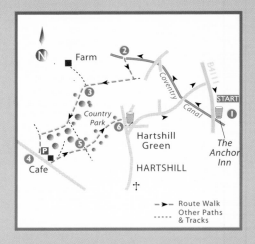

The Walk

① From the pub gain the towing path. Walk under the road bridge and continue with the water on your left side. Go under a road bridge then another by the waterway maintenance depot. At the next bridge (numbered 33) leave the waterway.

② Climb the steps to a stile and cross the canal. Walk over a field passing by an electricity pole and towards houses. On a rough vehicle track turn right. As the vehicle way twists right to a farm keep ahead over a stile. Walk over rough ground to a double step stile to woods.

③ Maintain the direction at the border of the woods. Ignore paths leading off and continue to a stile onto a fine stretch of grassland (picnic tables and benches). Turn left along a path beside the left-hand woods and continue to the car park.

④ Turn left. By the café and toilets take a path left. Go through a barrier and follow the clear path. Within a 100 yards the track divides – take the right-hand path. Drop steeply downhill and ignore other paths. In the valley and by a wide vehicle track turn left then at once right (by a post numbered 3).

⑤ Keep descending, past a waymark post. Cross a footbridge and keep ahead at post 4. Drop down steps to pass through a barrier. Walk along a raised causeway and

The Coventry Canal at Hartshill

climb steps to a road. Turn right to the little green and main road at Hartshill.

⑥ Cross to pass by a pub with the Michael Drayton bus shelter on your right. Within a short distance take a lane left. The narrow byway passes a junction then drops down to the B4111. Turn right to the pub.

PLACES OF INTEREST NEARBY

The **site of the Battle of Bosworth** is 6 miles along lanes to the north-east. This was the fateful battle of the Wars of the Roses in 1485. There are informative boards around a 1¼ mile long trail enabling one to trace the pattern of the battle in which Richard III fell leaving Henry Tudor to claim the throne. (Incidentally Richard was the last English monarch to die in battle.)

Fillongley
The Cottage Inn

MAP: OS LANDRANGER 140 (GR 277877) **WALK 2** **DISTANCE:** 3 MILES

DIRECTIONS TO START: FILLONGLEY IS ABOUT 6 MILES NORTH-WEST OF COVENTRY ALONG THE B4098. JUST NORTH OF THE VILLAGE, TURN OFF WESTWARDS, SIGNED TO THE PUB. **PARKING:** IN THE PUB CAR PARK.

The stroll from this rather isolated pub follows a brook through pastoral lands then nudges the hollows and ridges of one of Fillongley's two castles (both destroyed by Oliver Cromwell). The route then twists a way through mainly arable fields to the lane into the village. Nearby is what looks like a small church but closer examination reveals that the building has been skilfully converted into a house – the work was given a Civic Award in 1994. The 13th century church in the main street is a gem and an uncle of George Eliot is buried in the churchyard. This reminds us that this corner of Warwickshire is George Eliot country – she was born some 4 miles away at South Farm, Arbury. Another tablet (which mysteriously disappeared from the churchyard in 1940) was a Plague Stone which noted that 26 died of the disease in 1666. The final steps back to the pub are through delightful farmland.

The Cottage Inn

The pub is approached along a narrow country lane and has the appearance of a country cottage with a lovely garden overlooking the fields. Sitting outside for a summer barbecue (June to September) is wonderful on the right evening! The precise history is obscure but the old is obviously very old and tastefully blended with the modern additions.

The menu is very comprehensive and admirably away from the 'with chips' genre. By all means look at the specials board but try the Poached Breast of Chicken with Pink Grapefruit and Basil and you will not be disappointed and how good to see the cheeses are all excellent British varieties! The beers are Tetley, Boddingtons and Marston's plus a guest. The Cottage Inn is open daily from noon until 3 pm and 6 pm to 11 pm. Telephone: 01676 540599.

The Walk

① Out of the car park turn right along the lane. At the main road turn right to go over the little bridge. Cross the road and go along a house drive. As this bears right to the house keep ahead over a stile by a gate. Follow a vehicle way. Within 100 yards do not go over a wide bridge but turn right. Go over a stile to a meadow.

② Keep ahead alongside the stream on the left. Go through a corner gate and over a stile. Beyond a pipe is a bridge to cross the brook. Keep by the brook for another 100 yards then climb a rough fence stile on the left. Follow the green path.

③ At a vehicle drive turn left through a gate by a cottage. At once bear right along a farm tractor way. Through a gateway take a signed path right to walk alongside a right-hand hedge. Follow the edge of the field with the hidden brook now on the right. Go over a far corner stile. Keep the direction for a further 30 yards.

④ Look for a rather hidden bridge on the right. Over the water leave the brook (a castle site is nearby) and follow the right-hand boundary of a large field, going around corners to arrive eventually at a farm road. Turn right to the B4102.

⑤ Cross the road and turn right. Just before a farm take a signed path on the left. Walk by a barn and keep ahead at a signed meeting of paths. At a stile is a signed T-junction of paths. Climb the stile and at once turn right.

⑥ Follow the path alongside a right-hand hedge. Turn the far corner a few steps to a stile to a garden. Walk along the arrowed way to a lane. Turn right. About 100 yards past a phone box and a white house go through a hedge gap left. Follow the line of

The award-winning church conversion at Fillongley

the path (mind the nettles!) never far from the right-hand lane to a field. Keep ahead (right-hand hedge). In a corner (by a bungalow) maintain the heading through a coppice to another field. Aim to the left of an electricity pole then climb a stile to a recreation ground. Follow the path to a lane (church house nearby).

⑦ Turn left to the main road at Fillongley. Turn right and keep ahead at the crossroads. Opposite a garage climb a stile left. In this field and the next walk by the right-hand hedge to a distant double stile. Several paths are indicated; take the path right. Drop downhill and climb the corner stile. Join a farm track and cross a brook.

⑧ Walk at the right-hand border of the field and around corners to a stile by a farm. Over the stile turn right. Keeping the farm and a pool on the right continue to a lane by the farm drive. The Cottage Inn is a few steps to the right.

PLACES OF INTEREST NEARBY

Arbury Hall and gardens (4 miles east) are open Bank Holiday weekends (Sundays and Mondays) from Easter to September. The Hall is said to be the most complete surviving example of 18th century Gothic Revival in the country. It was George Eliot's 'Cheveral Manor' and South Farm (her birthplace) is on the estate. Telephone: 024 76382804. Nearby, at Nuneaton, there are further reminders of George Eliot where a park and buildings bear her name. Telephone Nuneaton Library for further details on 024 76384027.

Shilton
Ye Olde Plough

MAP: OS LANDRANGER 140 (GR 404845)   **WALK 3**   **DISTANCE:** 3 MILES

DIRECTIONS TO START: SHILTON IS 6 MILES NORTH-EAST OF COVENTRY, NOT FAR FROM THE M6/M69 INTERSECTION. APPROACHING FROM COVENTRY, TAKE THE A4600 THEN THE B4065 AND THE B4029 NORTHWARDS. THE PUB IS BY THE TRAFFIC LIGHTS IN THE CENTRE OF THE VILLAGE. **PARKING:** IN THE CAR PARK BESIDE THE PUB.

The M69 sears a way through the countryside of Shilton but one can soon escape from the noise along some attractive quiet byways. The first mile of the stroll is over arable lands to the village of Ansty. The imposing pedimented mansion of Ansty Hall was built in 1678 for a Roundhead leader, Richard Taylor. The nearby church has work of the 13th century. Then the walk is along a path beside the Oxford Canal; the waterway is popular with holiday boats today but when it was completed in 1790 after 30 years of construction the bargees complained of the slow twisting route. The Perpendicular tower of the 600-year-old Shilton church is our marker for the return to the village.

Ye Olde Plough

The road is busy through the village but the pub is fortunately off the main highway. This is a typical English village hostelry – unpretentious but giving a warm welcome to walkers. It has been a pub for as long anyone could remember; no doubt it was popular with the farm workers over the centuries as this has always been an intensive agricultural area.

A free house, the Olde Plough offers Marston's real ales and one can sit on the terrace in front of the inn where there is a pretty display of hanging baskets in summertime. The menu is modest but offers good value in traditional fare. I can especially recommend the steak and kidney pies and the ploughman's lunches. The pub is open from 11 am to 3 pm and from 6 pm to 11 pm with normal Sunday hours applying. Telephone: 024 76612402.

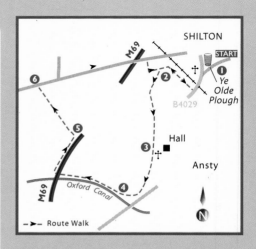

The Walk

① From the car park turn right. Keep ahead at the traffic lights to pass near the church. Go over the railway bridge and at once take a signed path at the side of a house. Keep ahead past a barrier along a hard path that soon borders an arable field.

The Oxford Canal

At the end of the field take a path left alongside a right-hand hedge.

② At the end of the hedge turn 90 degrees left with the path still bordering an arable field. After 200 yards climb a stile right. At once regain the old heading now in a pasture by a left-hand hedge. Nearing the church and the back of Ansty Hall (now a hotel) bear right.

③ Climb a stile to a vehicle way. Pass to the right of the church and walk through the churchyard to a stile to a meadow. Keep ahead to pick up a left-hand hedge. At the end of a house garden bear right to arrive at the canal.

④ Turn right. The footpath hugs the canal to reach a motorway bridge. Go under the highway and climb a stile to a pasture. Turn right to follow the edge of the motorway. Climb a corner stile and keep ahead.

⑤ At another corner of a field turn left so the hedge is on the right. Turn left for a few steps in the far corner to climb a stile by a metal gate. Walk up the slope alongside a right-hand hedge to a corner stile and a road.

⑥ Turn right and pass over the motorway. Just after the Shilton sign turn right down a signed path. A fenced way leads to a stile to an arable field. Follow the path to rejoin the outward route. Retrace your steps to the pub.

PLACES OF INTEREST NEARBY

About 4 miles south of Shilton along the B4029 and B4027 is **Coombe Countryside Park**. The park is in the grounds of Coombe Abbey which was founded by the Cistercian monks in 1150. It is administered by Coventry City Council and has fine gardens, walks and play areas. There are restaurant facilities.

Newbold-on-Avon
The Boat Inn

MAP: OS LANDRANGER 140 (GR 489773)   **WALK 4**   **DISTANCE:** 3½ MILES

DIRECTIONS TO START: APPROACHING FROM THE CENTRE OF RUGBY, TAKE THE A426. WITHIN ½ MILE GO UNDER A RAILWAY BRIDGE THEN IMMEDIATELY TAKE THE B4112 TO NEWBOLD. THE PUB IS ON THE RIGHT. **PARKING:** IN THE CAR PARK BESIDE THE PUB.

The start of the stroll is alongside the Oxford Canal. The waterway goes through a 400 yard tunnel – rather dark and eerie (or exciting for some) but you can cut out the canal walk to stay on a road if you wish! The bargees used to say you could hear the church clock strike all twenty-four hours because of the time it took to pass Newbold along the contour canal.

A delightfully typical English winding lane leads to Little Lawford. This hamlet used the waters of the Avon to power its mill (now a house); nearby is the Hall. Actually the great hall was pulled down in 1790 by the Caldecotts (after a murder!) and the Caldecotts built themselves Holbrook Grange.

After crossing the languid infant Avon there is a bridleway to Long Lawford. We pass the church that was primarily built in 1839 for the servants from the Grange. Over field paths another fine church is reached – dedicated to St Botolph, the patron saint of travellers.

The Boat Inn

This was a popular inn with the boat people on the nearby canal. Unpretentious outside, step through the door and there is a glorious miscellany of bric-à-brac. For example antique chamber pots vie for space with traditional painted canal pots and pans! There are prints of the old canal system and navigation maps – so much in this place to stimulate sagging conversation. The bars are cosy and floors boot-proof.

The 'superb home-cooked food' sign is indeed very apt. The menu is traditional with especially good pies. The beers available are Boddingtons and Marston's Pedigree. There are benches and tables to the front and rear of the pub to be sure to catch the sun. The pub is open all day, every day from 12 noon. Telephone: 01788 576995.

The Walk

① From the car park continue along the vehicle way to the canal. Turn left along the towing path with the water on your right side. Walk through the tunnel – there is a stout handrail to guide you. Emerging in the daylight climb steps left to a stile to a field. Turn right. Walk well to the right of the farm complex to a gate (tucked in a corner) to a road.

② Cross to the lane opposite. Follow the lane to Little Lawford. At the road junction turn left (signed to a ford).

③ Pass the Hall and continue around bends to the mill. Follow the vehicle way through a gate by the mill. Walk along a wide farm track to cross the River Avon. Keep ahead over a brook and through a metal gate and along the fenced way.

④ By houses go through a gate and walk along the road to pass the church of Long Lawford. Just beyond the church turn left along a vehicle way. As this twists sharp right go left through a metal kissing gate. The path is signed through a churchyard then through another gate.

⑤ In a ridge and furrow field turn right. Continue over the field (wood on the right) then another to cross a bridge spanning a brook. Bear right along a clear path over sheep pastures to a far step stile. Follow the path between houses to an estate road.

⑥ Bear slightly left to the next path between houses numbered 20 and 22. Go over a step stile to a meadow and follow the well-used

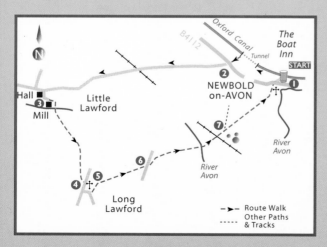

The bridge over the languid River Avon

track over the open field. Climb a stile to the following field and maintain the heading to another stile. Continue to a raised metal causeway and over a rather elegant metal bridge. Keep the direction through a gate to a farm drive and under the railway.

⑦ When the farm drive twists left keep ahead along a clear path through rough scrubland. Go over an old bridge and through a gate. Walk along an avenue of oaks to a far stile into a churchyard. Turn left with the church on the right side to a road. The pub is to the right.

PLACES OF INTEREST NEARBY

Just down the road from Newbold-on-Avon is **Rugby.** The famous school was founded in 1567 and this is where the game of rugby originated. The school moved to the central site in the middle of the 18th century. At 5, Hillmorton Road an old boy Rupert Brooke was born.

Hockley Heath
The Wharf Tavern

MAP: OS LANDRANGER 139 (GR 152724) · **WALK 5** · **DISTANCE:** 4 MILES

DIRECTIONS TO START: HOCKLEY HEATH IS ON THE A3400 10 MILES SOUTH OF BIRMINGHAM. THE PUB IS AT THE SOUTH END OF THE VILLAGE BY THE CANAL BRIDGE. **PARKING:** IN THE CAR PARK BEHIND THE PUB.

The first mile or so of the walk from the Wharf Tavern is beside the tranquil waters of the Stratford-upon-Avon Canal. This waterway was a busy commercial artery delivering coal south and limestone and agricultural goods northwards. Nowadays the fun sailors ply these waters and you are sure to meet numerous holiday craft in summertime. There are many distinctive features including barrel-roofed lock-keepers' cottages, draw-bridges and split bridges to allow horses' tow ropes to pass through. The paths then lead through pastures to the village of Lapworth; this is a scattered community with an elusive centre – perhaps to keep it the rather exclusive place that it is! It was certainly a secret place for one of its sons – the Gunpowder Plot conspirator Robert Catesby.

We pass Lapworth's lovely hilltop church with a graceful spire then descend to a tributary of the little River Tapster. (Lovers of quiet places were unsuccessful in stopping a motorway through the valley!) The return to Hockley Heath nudges the parkland of Umberslade Hall with its little obelisk.

The Wharf Tavern

This pub had its wharf restored a short time ago after sixty years of neglect; it was here that coal and commercial cargoes were unloaded and distributed to a wide area. Now the holiday craft can moor alongside the pub's gardens. What I like at this place are the many little alcoves around the bars where you can have that quiet tête-à-tête. On the walls are fascinating prints of the canal in days long ago. The food here is traditional pub fare – often specialising in 'roasts of the day'. Puds too are for those starting their dieting on the morrow – just try the spotted dick and custard first! There is also a Children's Carvery and plenty of veggie meals. The opening hours are 11 am to 3 pm and 6 pm to 11 pm but tend to be longer at weekends. Telephone: 01564 782075.

The Walk

① From the car park go to the canal towing path. Turn left and go over the little bridge by the wharf. Continue along the towing path to go under the main road with the water on your right side. Stay by the canal for about 1¹⁄₂ miles.

② At bridge number 30 leave the canal. Cross the water and at once go through a kissing gate. Follow the border of a cricket ground to a stile. Do not climb this but turn 90 degrees right. Cross a rough pasture to another stile. Maintain the heading to climb a far stile. Walk by a left-hand pool and follow a clear path at the end of a garden. Climb a stile and maintain the direction to a stile onto a lane.

③ Turn right then left by the war memorial. Opposite the church go over a stile and take the indicated direction to drop down the vale. Keep ahead over a stile and go over the ridge. Again drop downhill to a stile and bridge over a brook. Bear slightly right to walk to a kissing gate under an oak tree. (Note – not to the corner stile to the left.)

④ Turn right through the gate. Within 200 yards and by a little fence bear half left over the field. The path then borders a left-hand fence. Continue to a stile onto a lane.

⑤ Turn right. After about 50 yards take a signed path left. Go through bushes and continue to a dump area (old tyres etc). Twist left along a cart track and walk to a stile to a main road.

⑥ Cross then turn left for a couple of steps to a rather hidden stile. Walk along a fenced way to a grassy

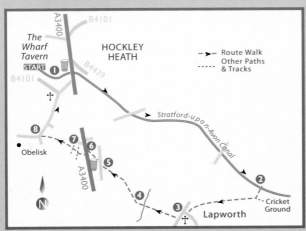

The Stratford-upon-Avon Canal

paddock. Bear right to a stile onto a vehicle way. Turn right then left to go around the end of a white building to a stile now seen.

⑦ Two paths are now signed. Go directly over the house drive to a pasture. Walk the length of the field. Go through a metal gate and climb a stile. Take a way slightly left of the arrowed direction to drop down to a gate to a lane.

⑧ Turn right. Pass a junction and climb the hill to the B4101. Turn right then left at the A3400 to the pub.

PLACES OF INTEREST NEARBY

Well signed from Hockley Heath and 2 miles along the B4439 is the National Trust's **Packwood House**. The 16th century house is fine but what is unique here is the splendid topiary garden which is said to portray the Sermon on the Mount. The property is open from the end of March to the end of September. Telephone: 01564 782024.

Wood End
The Old Royal Oak

MAP: OS LANDRANGER 139 (GR 107718)	WALK 6	DISTANCE: 2 MILES

DIRECTIONS TO START: WOOD END IS ON THE B4101 ROAD BETWEEN HOCKLEY HEATH AND REDDITCH. THE PUB IS BY THE STATION. **PARKING:** IN THE CAR PARK BESIDE THE PUB.

This stroll is between the hamlet of Wood End and the village of Tanworth-in-Arden. The paths go through a gentle pastoral landscape and cross a railway that has led a charmed life. Since the days of the infamous Beeching cuts it has been threatened with closure many times but still survives.

Tanworth is a remarkably isolated village devoid of any main road. There is a lovely amalgam of different building styles and a hilltop landmark church beside the village green where there is a 'spreading chestnut tree'. There are still village shops, but look at the names of the old houses which indicate the extent of commerce in past days – there is the Old Boot Shop, Cobbler's Cottage, the Old Bank House and so on. The village was originally the Saxon Tanewotha or 'the thane's worth'.

The Old Royal Oak

'Royal Oak' appears in the name of over five hundred English pubs – a popular name commemorating Charles II's exploits after the Battle of Worcester (1651) when he hid in an oak tree and then avoided capture by fleeing around the countryside. Wood End's Old Royal Oak is rather up-market but welcomes ramblers, locals and travellers to a cosy bar (there are a few stools but it is mainly for standing customers) and restaurant. The sun trap garden is a delight on warm days.

The starters in themselves are substantial meals here. Try the grilled black pudding – a traditional Midlands dish – coated in a grain mustard sauce with roasted pinenuts or the poached eggs served on toasted brioche with bacon and hollandaise sauce. In Victorian times the regulations decreed that the place (then the Royal Oak Inn) could stay open while there was still an empty bed – needless to say it was never a problem to ensure that the beer pumps were kept going! The real ales served from those pumps today are Bass, Tetley and a guest. The opening hours are 11 am to 3 pm and 5.30 pm to 11 pm on Monday to Friday and all day opening at the weekends. Telephone: 01564 742346.

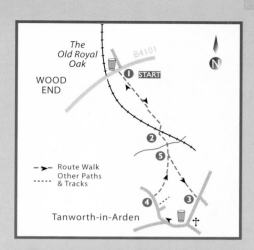

The Walk

① Directly opposite the pub take a signed path down a vehicle way. Go past the entrance to houses and keep ahead to walk along a fenced footpath through woods to a step stile. In the pasture take an indicated direction to a gate to cross the railway.

② Over the railway bear left to a rather hidden footbridge over a brook by oak trees. Climb the stile to a meadow. Bear left to a stile (the left one of two). Follow the arrowed direction of the path. Over a far corner stile keep the heading to emerge on a lane to the left of houses and a metal gate.

③ Turn right on the road which you follow through the village past the church, inn and post-office. Go by the Ivy Stores and keep ahead at a junction. Note the whalebone arch of an aptly-named cottage.

④ Just past an estate road (on the right) ignore one signed footpath. A few yards further take another path. Walk at the side of a garden. In a pasture follow the right-

PLACES OF INTEREST NEARBY

At Tanworth-in-Arden is the **Umberslade Children's Farm**. This is a delightful 'hands-on' visit for youngsters with a fine assortment of farm animals and a tour of the countryside on a cart behind a tractor is fun. Open daily. Telephone: 01564 742251.

Tanworth-in-Arden

hand hedge to a stile tucked in a corner. Beyond, continue by a left-hand hedge to a corner stile.

⑤ Join the outward route and retrace your steps over the railway to the Old Royal Oak.

Kenilworth
The Clarendon Arms

MAP: OS LANDRANGER 139 AND 140 (GR 280723)

WALK 7

DISTANCE: 3½ MILES

DIRECTIONS TO START: THE PUB IS AT CASTLE GREEN NEAR THE CASTLE ON THE WEST SIDE OF KENILWORTH AND IS REACHED ON THE B4103. **PARKING:** THERE IS NO PUB CAR PARK BUT USE THE PUBLIC PARK OUTSIDE THE NEARBY CASTLE WALLS.

The walk is along well-waymarked paths. It starts outside the walls of the great castle which was begun by Geoffrey de Clinton in 1125. He liked the site on a huge rocky outcrop – so did the covetous Henry II who took possession and built the large keep. King John spent £2,000 on the place. John of Gaunt, Duke of Lancaster, changed Kenilworth from a severe fortress into a magnificent mansion. Cromwell decreed that it should become a ruin to stop it being used for future conflicts.

The stroll continues beside meadows that were once covered with water – the Pool added to the defensive strength of the castle. A short lane stretch crosses a ford – Inchford Brook was dammed to provide water to the Pool. The return to Kenilworth is along pleasant fieldpaths – with every step the massive fortification becomes ever more impressive.

The Clarendon Arms

The Clarendon Arms is cheek by jowl with another pub but holds its own with its value for money meals (the sausages and burgers are modestly described as 'probably the best in Warwickshire') and friendly ambience. So who were the noble Clarendons? Lord Clarendon was Chief Minister to Charles II and the monarch gave him the nearby castle as a gift. It was a little wanted ruin – only the stones were considered of value. The pub went with the castle until 1937 and was always a real basic drinking place for the farm workers of Castle Green. The size of the narrow building is deceptive – it has been greatly extended to the rear.

There is a wonderful choice of real ales to please the beer connoisseur – take your choice from Courage, John Smith's, Ansells, Morland and a guest such as the popular M&B Brew XI. There are plenty of 'snug' corners in the bars and a pleasant small patio. My Meg spotted the 'No Dogs' sign. Opening hours are 11am to 3 pm and 5.30pm to 11pm Monday to Saturday and all day on Sunday from 12 noon. Telephone: 01926 852017.

The Walk

① From the car park take the path that runs beside the castle walls. Keep the walls then railings on your right. Climb steps to a wide vehicle track – the way into the castle. Cross the track and go down steps. Turn left along a path with a ruined wall on your side to a step stile.

② Climb the stile to meadows where the great Pool once covered the grass. Keep near the left-hand border of the field. Go

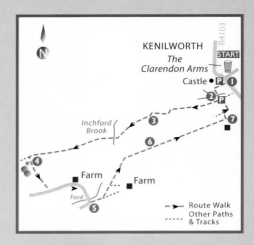

over a corner stile and keep ahead to climb another stile then another (with triple steps) tucked in a corner.

③ Bear left alongside a left-hand hedge to climb a hidden corner stile. Follow the path over the open field to cross Inchford Brook. Beyond keep the direction over the open field. Climb a stile and keep ahead to a further stile under an oak tree. Still ahead (open field) go through a hedge gap (superfluous stile) and maintain the direction, aiming to the right of a row of oaks.

④ At a waymark post several paths are arrowed. Turn left (oaks now on the right). Follow the tractor way up the rise to a stile. Beyond, walk over the open field to another stile onto a lane. Turn left and cross the ford.

⑤ As the lane twists sharp right go left along the drive of Fernhill Farm. Within 200 yards go through a hedge gap to the left. Follow the clear path over the field to the far side. Keep the old heading through a wide hedge gap. In a far corner climb a

Kenilworth Castle

rather hidden step stile. Turn right alongside a right-hand fence and hedge.

⑥ At a stile change fields. Regain the old heading, now by a left-hand hedge. Climb a corner stile and maintain the bearing over a similar corner stile.

⑦ Keep ahead to emerge on a vehicle way with a house on the right. Turn left over a stile by a cattle grid. Keep along the vehicle way to a car park. Turn left over the bridge above the old moat, walking towards the castle entrance. Drop down the steps climbed earlier and retrace the way by the walls to the car park.

PLACES OF INTEREST NEARBY

Allow time to visit **Kenilworth Castle**. It is possible to see the spectacular ruins including the keep and battlements. In recent years a Tudor garden has been created. The castle is open daily throughout the year. Telephone: 01926 852078. In a park opposite the pub are the **ruins of an Augustinian priory**. Like the castle it was founded by Geoffrey de Clinton. It became an abbey in the middle of the 15th century.

Frankton
The Friendly Inn

DIRECTIONS TO START: FRANKTON IS A RATHER REMOTE VILLAGE SOUTH-EAST
OF COVENTRY. TURN SOUTH-WEST OFF THE A45 ONTO THE B4453 THEN TAKE
SIGNED LANES TO FRANKTON. THE PUB IS IN THE CENTRE OF THE VILLAGE.
PARKING: IN THE CAR PARK BEHIND THE PUB.

We are rarely out of view of Frankton's church on the first section of the route. The parish church of St Nicholas dates back to the 13th century and one of the doors has been swinging on its hinges for almost 700 years! Alongside the church since 1662 has been the Manor House – the Biddulph family were here for over 300 years but are now only remembered in street names.

The walk then is along lanes and fieldpaths to Bourton on Dunsmore. This was once an estate village; the Great Hall was in ruins until rescued in 1979 by an industrial firm. We pass the old Free School (built in 1847 by John Shuckburgh) and the octagonal building which was once a tollhouse then a laundry for the Hall. Lanes take us back to the pub at Frankton.

The Friendly Inn

Although the building has been a pub for as long as anyone can remember, it was once a farmhouse; there are three distinct parts to the place. Beside the house was the cattle shed and at the end were the stables. Locals recall when all the customers were mainly farm workers from the village – no car park was needed and the site was used for chicken pens. The population of Frankton is still only about 300 so the Friendly Inn does now rely on its reputation to attract 'outsiders' although it is said that much of the village entertainment is held here. There are regular quizzes and pub games like skittles and darts are played.

Good old English beef is a mainstay of the menu with the Steak Diane and Côte de Boeuf highly praised – as are the veggie meals like home-made Mediterranean Vegetable Pie. Beers on offer include Ruddles, Greene King IPA and Ansells. For those hazy, lazy days of summer there is a new patio. The opening hours are 12 noon to 3 pm and 6 pm to 11 pm. Telephone: 01926 632430.

Frankton

The Walk

① Out of the car park turn left along Fair Close. At a meeting of lanes keep ahead along a lane signed as a no through road. Just after a farmhouse and barn on the right take a path over a stile on the left.

② In a sheep pasture take a direction aiming towards a far farm complex. Pass through a hunting gate next to a field gate onto a lane. Turn left then right at a crossroads (the lane to Birdingbury).

③ Within ¼ mile turn left through a hunting gate and walk along a signed bridle-way.

④ At a lane turn right.

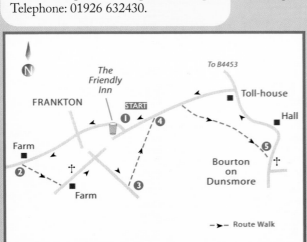

The impressive gates to the Hall at Bourton on Dunsmore

Within 400 yards take a path signed through a gate right. Walk by a left-hand hedge to a gateway (no gate). Do not go through but take a path bearing left. Walk along a twisting grassed way to a field. Take the arrowed way over the open field. Pass through a hedge gap and take the indicated direction half right to a gap in the far right-hand corner of the field. Follow the fenced way to a lane at Bourton on Dunsmore.

⑤ Turn left. Pass the elegant gates to the Hall and the old school. At a junction is the former tollhouse. Turn left; the lane leads back to Frankton and the pub.

PLACES OF INTEREST NEARBY

Ryton Pools are 5 miles north-west of Frankton along the B4453, A423 and A445. The area was once riddled with unsightly sand and gravel pits; they then became even more unsightly rubbish dumps. When the site could take no more rubbish the imaginative plan to turn the area into a large country park took root. The Ryton Pools Country Park was opened in 1996 with picnic areas, lakes and woods. There is also a little power station which uses the methane gas from the buried rubbish. Telephone: 01827 872660 for details.

Henley-in-Arden
The Nag's Head

MAP: OS LANDRANGER 151 (GR 152659)   **WALK 9**   **DISTANCE:** 2½ MILES

DIRECTIONS TO START: HENLEY-IN-ARDEN IS ON THE A3400 15 MILES SOUTH OF BIRMINGHAM. THE PUB IS IN THE MAIN STREET JUST SOUTH OF THE PARISH CHURCH. **PARKING:** THERE IS A CAR PARK THROUGH THE ARCH AT THE SIDE OF THE PUB.

Henley-in-Arden is an attractive starting place especially in summertime when you can marvel at the street floral displays – the town often wins well-deserved awards. The mile long main street has buildings of all styles of many centuries each rubbing eaves delightfully with their neighbours. Near the pub is the parish church dated 1448; within a few hundred yards down a lane is the even earlier Beaudesert church. Why two churches? The answer perhaps is that the little river between them would flood and the road become impassable. Next to the parish church is the Guild Hall where the meetings of the Court Leet and Court Baron are still held.

The walk follows a railway (miraculously saved from the Beecham axe) then borders a golf course. The route goes through pastoral lands then climbs the ridge to reward you with splendid views. The final climb is up the strategic hill on which Thurstan de Montfort built his great castle; its fortunes declined after the Battle of Evesham.

The Nag's Head

The history of this pub is something of a puzzle. There is an archway at the side which seems to suggest an entrance for horses and carriages and therefore a coaching inn, but none of the locals talked of this. The age indicated by the outside belies the interior – the oak beams are truly ancient and gargantuan, and look up at the height of the bar ceiling. One local thought the pub was once much smaller and was joined to the next door cottage to expand the bar. This is a typical old-type town pub – nothing flamboyant but offering genuine olde worlde hospitality. There is a real stone-flagged floor and the oak furnishings have no place for plastic imitations. Opening hours are 11 am to 11 pm Monday to Saturday and from 12 noon to 11 pm on Sunday.

The real ales sold are Ansells but there is always a guest – Timothy Taylor Golden Best on my visit. Kids are welcome – but sadly my Meg was barred even in the large garden that attractively borders the River Alne. Food is quite standard but good; I was drawn to the Pork and Gravy Baguette. The many mottoes on the beams are intriguing – among them Housman's 'And malt does more than Milton can – to justify God's way to man'. Telephone: 01564 792621.

The Walk

① Out of the car park and into the High Street cross and turn right. Just past another pub (the White Swan) turn left – signed as being on the route of the Heart of England Way.

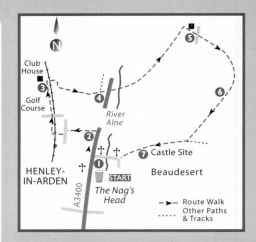

② Keep ahead past Shallowford Court and the head of an estate road. Follow the path to Station Road. Cross to the path opposite to go over the railway bridge. Immediately turn right on the path beside the railway. Cross a vehicle way and climb the steps. Go over a stile and (still by the railway) continue alongside a golf course.

③ At a vehicle way near the clubhouse turn right. Go over the railway. The vehicle way bears left. About 300 yards later the way twists sharply left again. Keep ahead over a step stile and along a hard path to a stile onto the main road.

④ Cross almost directly over. Follow the winding path to cross the river. Pass through a kissing gate and keep the direction over a pasture (never far from the right-hand border) to a rough stile. Still maintain the direction over a meadow, aiming to the left of a distant house. Pick up a left-hand hedge and continue to a far corner stile in a wire fence. Turn right to pass the house. Continue by the wire fence to a rough stile onto a lane.

The Guild Hall, Henley-in-Arden

⑤ Turn right. Go between two brick walls (once a railway bridge). Immediately take a signed path left that leads to a field. Go directly across to a rather hidden stile tucked in a corner to the left of a gateway. Go half right to climb along a faint path to the right-hand end of the ridge.

⑥ Go over a stile then follow the clear path along the ridge. We pick up the route of the Heart of England Way. Go through a gateway after about ⅓ mile and take the arrowed direction right to drop downhill. Keeping the direction, climb to the old castle site.

⑦ Still on the same heading go down the hill to pass through a gate to a lane near the Norman Beaudesert church. Follow the lane over the river to Henley's High Street. The Nag's Head is a few steps left.

PLACES OF INTEREST NEARBY

About 7 miles north-east along the A3400, B4439 and signed lanes is the moated medieval manor house of **Baddesley Clinton**. This romantic National Trust property has changed little since 1634. There are several priest's holes and delightful gardens. The house is open from March to November but phone first to get details. Telephone: 01564 783294.

Claverdon
The Crown Inn

MAP: OS LANDRANGER 151 (GR 196650)   **WALK 10**   **DISTANCE:** 3½ MILES

DIRECTIONS TO START: CLAVERDON IS ON THE A4189 6 MILES WEST OF WARWICK. THE CROWN INN IS AT THE WEST END OF THE VILLAGE. **PARKING:** THERE IS A LARGE CAR PARK AT THE SIDE OF THE PUB.

The walk starts with a short road section then there are quiet footpaths to Yarningale Common, one of the few commons in the county. (Most commons like this one are privately owned and were the areas in medieval times – often the poorer soils – where the lord of the manor allowed the commoners to graze animals and grow crops.) Beyond the common (on which a small Iron Age fort was perched) we reach the Stratford-upon-Avon Canal. This waterway was used to convey coal southwards and limestone in the opposite direction. Today the captains and their crews man the pleasure craft to and from the Midlands and the Avon.

Claverdon was once 'cloverdown' and has many delightful corners of thatched cottages and old buildings like the Forge and the National School building of 1847, now an up-market house.

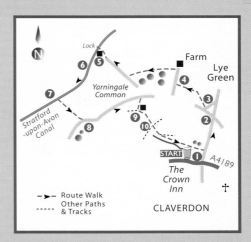

The Crown Inn

The building belies its age – it was 1750 when the place was constructed and it was once a butcher's shop. This is a fine community pub, popular with sportsmen and very actively supporting its favourite charity – the Guide Dogs for the Blind.

The landlady is rightly proud of Irene's Sizzlers – a more than ample steak or grill – with those naughty chips too! Specials of the Day are displayed on a board near the bar. The real ales are the regular Brew XI and a guest. Although there is a cosy restaurant this is basically still a village pub. It is open all day at the weekend; on Monday to Friday the hours are 11.30 am to 2.30 pm and 5.30 pm to 11 pm. Telephone: 01926 842210.

The Walk

① Turn left out of the car park then left at the crossroads and little village green with the spreading chestnut tree. The road leads to the hamlet of Lye Green.

② Turn left (signed to Yarningale Common) at the crossroads. The green is now on your right. Just past a post-box and junction a path is signed on the right.

③ Go over a stile then another to a field. Take the arrowed direction to a stile in a fence. Keep the heading over the open field to another stile. Walk on to a corner stile. Follow the path alongside a right-hand hedge to a wood. Keep ahead to a lane.

④ Turn right. At the end and by a farm turn left along a vehicle way. We now follow a way never far from the border of the woodlands along paths and vehicle tracks and by houses to a tarmac lane. Turn right.

⑤ At the end of the lane the next path is signed at the right-hand side of a cream-coloured house. Continue to the canal and cross the water. Nearby is one of the distinctive barrel-roofed lock-keepers' cottages. Turn left along the towing path.

⑥ Go past bridge 45. (Note the slit down the crown of the bridge to obviate the need to unhitch the towing ropes of the horses.) At bridge 46 cross the water.

⑦ At once leave the canal by going through the metal gate and into a field. Turn right and walk over the open field, aiming for the left-hand corner of a distant wood. Go through a metal hunting gate and continue to a lane.

⑧ Turn left. Go past signed paths and continue to Yarningale Common. Just before a road junction and by a car park turn right down a rough vehicle way.

⑨ At the end several paths are signed.

Meg outside the lock-keeper's cottage

Turn left (there are kennels on the left) and climb a stile. Walk along a clear path over rough grass to a stile by a metal gate. Proceed to a corner stile. Follow the arrowed direction over the open field to a stile.

⑩ Several paths are signed. Keep ahead along a bridleway. Within 200 yards leave the main way by taking a signed path over a plank bridge right. The path borders a right-hand stream. Continue to a far right-hand corner of the field then walk along a fenced path to a road at Claverdon. Retrace your steps to the pub.

PLACES OF INTEREST NEARBY

Hatton Country World and Craft Village is reached along the road towards Warwick. Take a signed left hand lane. The Centre has a fascinating array of craft shops and animals in a farm setting. There is also a nature trail and café. Telephone: 01926 843411.

Long Itchington
The Two Boats Inn

MAP: OS LANDRANGER 151 (GR 417647) | **WALK 11** | **DISTANCE:** 2 MILES

DIRECTIONS TO START: LONG ITCHINGTON IS 10 MILES SOUTH OF COVENTRY ON THE A423 BANBURY ROAD. THE PUB IS TO THE SOUTH OF THE VILLAGE BY THE CANAL BRIDGE. **PARKING:** IN THE PUB CAR PARK.

The first mile of this short walk is along the towing path of the Grand Union Canal. This waterway was the M1 of its day, carrying freight between London and Birmingham. It was the amalgamation of eight smaller canals but did not fully become one company until 1929. With the incorrect belief that there was a great future in the movement of freight by water and assisted by Government grants a major widening scheme was undertaken in the 1930s necessitating the rebuilding of many locks and what has been called 'marvels of engineering'. Now as you walk the chances are that several pleasure craft will pass as this is now a popular holiday route.

After the stroll along the towpath there are fieldpaths across arable lands and beside the little River Itchen which gives the village its name. Gradually the church tower comes into view across the meadows. The church is mainly 14th century but Long Itchington's most famous son was the Saxon bishop St Wulfstan.

The Two Boats Inn

In all likelihood this was a pub established to serve the wants of the bargees on the busy canal and down below there was a forge to shoe the towing horses. This pub sits on one bank with another pub on the opposite bank – not glaring across the water at its rival as the two landlords are friends. (The other pub has play contraptions for youngsters which does somewhat sort out the clientele!)

Although the Two Boats' bars are beamed and cosy it is very pleasant to sit outside by the towing path under gay umbrellas on warm days. Dogs if on their good behaviour are welcome. There are always four real ales on offer including Bass, Abbot Ale and Worthington. For food the specials board is worth studying but the 'Fillet' (a steak with smoked bacon topped with melted Stilton) is a popular choice. There is always a variety of veggie meals on offer. The pub is open everyday from 12 noon to 11 pm. Telephone: 01926 812640.

The Walk

① From the front of the pub go along the towing path under the road bridge. Go under a farm bridge then the bridge of a long-abandoned rail route. At bridge 27 leave the waterway. Go up steps to a lane.

② Turn right. Within 200 yards cross the lane to a signed footpath through a hedge gap. Walk directly away from the road for 100 yards then turn 90 degrees right. Walk over the open field to a path through a coppice. Drop downhill then pass through a kissing gate to cross the old rail route.

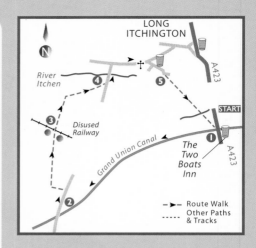

③ Climb steps to another kissing gate onto pastures. Walk alongside a right-hand hedge. Over a corner stile take a path signed to the right. Follow a way near the right-hand border of the rough pasture to cross a stile and bridge tucked in a corner. Follow the arrowed way to a stile onto a lane.

④ Turn left to cross the little River Itchen. At a T-junction turn right to Long Itchington. Pass the church to reach the square. Turn right. Around a bend climb a stile by a gateway on the right.

PLACES OF INTEREST NEARBY

Draycote Water Country Park is 5 miles along lanes and the A426 north-east of Long Itchington. Based on the man-made (1972) reservoir (water is pumped from the River Leam) the water covers over 600 acres. Fishermen can try for trout here. There are walkways by the reservoir where you can observe the wildfowl and sailing craft; large grassy areas are fine for games and picnics and there is a café nearby. Telephone: 01827 872660 for details.

Long Itchington

⑤ In the field take the arrowed direction. Pass well to the left of a telegraph post to a far stile. On the same heading cross the bridge over a brook. Now aim to the left of a distant chimney to cross a vehicle drive. Continue to a corner and the road. Nearby is the pub.

Haseley
The Falcon

MAP: OS LANDRANGER 151 (GR 232679)   **WALK 12**   DISTANCE: 3½ MILES

DIRECTIONS TO START: THE PUB IS 3½ MILES NORTH-WEST OF WARWICK ON THE EAST SIDE OF THE A4177. **PARKING:** THE LARGE CAR PARK IS TO THE REAR OF THE PUB.

The stroll starts along short fieldpaths and passes rather elegant houses where we can admire the fine gardens. The next stretch is beside the Grand Union Canal which was one of the most important routes of the Canal Age, taking goods to and from the Midlands (see also Walk 11).

At a crossroads is a rather fine former school building carrying the initials AH – was it Mr Hewlett (a mining engineer at the Manor House), I wonder, who gave it to the village in 1924? We have a view of the Manor across the fields – a Tudor-style mansion but built in 1875. Before the last fieldpath is the gem-of-a-church overlooking the fields. Note the interesting Throckmorton brasses – the family lived at the Manor.

The Falcon

I like the Falcon; it is openly hospitable and is rightly proud to say so! For example a 'Happy Hour', a 'Children are Welcome' notice, 'Rediscover the Country Pub' and 'Widest ever choice of vegetarian meals' signs and so on. The building probably started life as a working farm, then (being well placed on the main highway west of Warwick) was a coaching inn. There are many old prints around the bar and (apart from motors taking the place of bicycles and horses) does not appear to have changed its exterior for over a hundred years. The locals still talk of a recent landlord Tom Dollery who had great success in cricket both for Warwickshire and England.

The real ales on offer are Banks's Bitter, Hook Norton, Brew XI, Marston's Pedigree and a guest. There is a full menu with 'Specials of the Day' but the bar snacks are quite substantial. For the figure conscious the summer salads are delightful but the 'with chips' dishes are a temptation! There is a large garden for use when the sun shines. The pub is open on Monday to Saturday from 11.30 am to 11 pm and on Sunday from 12 noon to 10.30 pm. Telephone 01926 484737.

The Walk

① From the car park proceed to the main road. Turn right along the pavement for 100 yards. Cross to the signed path beside cottages and go down a vehicle way. Keep to the right of a fence, walking at the side of the field. At a corner of the fence keep ahead over the open field. Aim towards a distant stile. (Note – the waymark arrow is a little awry.)

② Over the stile turn right along the lane. Within 250 yards and just past a cottage take a signed path down a vehicle drive left. Within a few steps climb a stile on the right. Follow the path at the left-hand side of the field. Cross a lane and take the indicated direction through paddock fields where horses graze.

③ Climb a corner stile. Follow a house drive passing a house called 'The Croft'. By a gateway (Shrewley Fields) climb a stile and keep ahead then (still the same direction) take a fenced path beside a Severn Trent Water Station. Follow the fenced way and climb stiles to the B4439.

④ Cross the road and turn left. Ignore a footpath sign on the right. After 300 yards of roadside walking take a path almost opposite the entrance to a garden centre. Over the stile take the arrowed direction over sheeplands to a high stile in a wire

Haseley village hall

fence. Keep the heading over the next pasture to a far corner stile onto a lane.

⑤ Turn right and continue until you cross the canal. At once pass through a little gate on the right to join the towing path. Walk under the road. At the next bridge (numbered 55) climb the steps to a lane. Turn left to go over the canal.

⑥ Keep ahead at the crossroads with the B4439 to another crossroads with the A4177. (The old school is nearby and the Manor across the fields.) Cross to the lane opposite. The lane goes to Haseley church.

⑦ Just before the church take a signed bridleway on the left. Follow the track at the side of the field to the pub car park.

PLACES OF INTEREST NEARBY

A mile towards Warwick along the B4177 turn right to the car park beside the canal. There is an interesting information display about the canal – here is the famous **Hatton Flight** with its 21 locks over only 2 miles lifting the water to 337 ft above sea level. (Hard work for the holiday sailors especially as the gates are so large!)

Bearley
The Golden Cross

MAP: OS LANDRANGER 151 (GR 170610) **WALK 13** **DISTANCE:** 3½ MILES

DIRECTIONS TO START: BEARLEY CROSS IS 4 MILES NORTH OF STRATFORD-UPON-AVON ON THE A3400. THE PUB IS AT THE CROSSROADS. **PARKING:** THERE IS A CAR PARK AT THE SIDE OF THE PUB.

This stroll shows us a variety of travel trails that so typify our landscape. The railway which we cross came to these parts in 1908; the North Warwickshire line has been under threat of closure for many decades but sense prevails and the tracks still relieve the main road (which fortunately we avoid!).

The placid waterway is the Stratford-upon-Avon Canal. This was fully completed in 1816 but for many years was un-navigable. It too was due officially to be closed but enthusiasts assisted the National Trust to save it. Today it is one of the most popular waterways for inland boat enthusiasts.

In addition, of course, we stroll along some delightful bridleways and footpaths from the village of Bearley. Bearley's church was lovingly restored 40 years ago without masking its Norman work. Village folklore tells of the miller who hid his gold under a huge millstone. It is unattended in the full moon at midnight but no young man so far has had the strength to lift the stone. Dare I mention a JCB?

Then we are told that Charles II passed the inn at Bearley Cross with Mistress Lane on the pillion when fleeing from Worcester. Fortunately they narrowly missed a troop of horse!

The Golden Cross

This 400-year-old busy little inn was even busier during the war. Just down the road was Snitterfield RAF station which was built for bombers. The landlord is proud to show photos of the airmen enjoying their off-duty time at the pub. (Today you can learn to fly gliders or play golf on the airfield site.) There are also prints dated 1908 showing the place in peaceful times with the horses and carriages outside.

The real ales on offer are Boddingtons and Flowers Original. The menu is modest but still offers a nice choice. The half roast duckling in a Calvados sauce is large enough to make walking **before** partaking advisable! Opening hours are 11 am to 2.30 pm and 6 pm to 11 pm on Monday to Saturday with normal Sunday hours applying. Telephone: 01789 731250.

The Walk

① From the car park turn right along the A3400. Go under the railway. At a junction bear left along the lane signed to Bearley. Go by the new village hall.

② About 100 yards before the church gate turn right along Ash Lane. Past cottages

An aqueduct on the Stratford-upon-Avon canal

the lane becomes a wide cart track signed as a bridleway. At a waymark post keep ahead along the bridleway (blue arrow) through an elongated wood. Continue to the main road.

③ Cross the road and turn left. Within 30 yards climb steps right. Up the bank a signed path starts. Walk over the open field directly away from the main road aiming for a solitary oak tree. Bearing slightly right follow the line of trees (the old hedge line). At the end of a hedge veer slightly left over the open field towards another oak. Keep ahead to a crossing place of the railway.

④ Maintain the heading across a brook and the rough ground beyond. At a bold path turn left to a canal bridge.

⑤ Turn right along the towing path. Keep by the canal for about a mile. At bridge 57 take a path right. In the field follow a way near the left-hand border to a lane. The fine high canal aqueduct is to the left but we go right – the lane leads back to the Golden Cross.

PLACES OF INTEREST NEARBY

At weekends it is fun to watch the activities at **Snitterfield Gliding Club**. Just off the A3400 towards Stratford-upon-Avon is **Mary Arden's House** in Wilmcote. Mary Arden was the mother of Shakespeare and the house contains a fine assortment of country artefacts. Telephone: 01789 293455.

Napton-on-the-Hill
The King's Head

MAP: OS LANDRANGER 151 (GR 466619) | **WALK 14** | **DISTANCE:** 3½ MILES

DIRECTIONS TO START: NAPTON-ON-THE-HILL IS JUST OFF THE A425 SOUTHAM TO DAVENTRY ROAD. THE KING'S HEAD IS AT THE A425 CROSSROADS ON THE NORTHERN OUTSKIRTS OF THE VILLAGE. **PARKING:** IN THE PUB CAR PARK.

The stroll is up the high hill of the village then around the bends of the Oxford Canal. The village (appropriately named from the Saxon 'settlement on a hilltop') was once the third largest town in the county, possessing three manors and granted that all-important medieval right by Edward II to hold fairs and markets.

On the walk we see two splendid buildings on the hilltop. The church which is some way from the villagers is dedicated to St Lawrence. It has a history going back to the 13th century. The tower gazes over the finely restored windmill which was built in 1543. Then fieldpaths lead over the pastures to the waterway. The Oxford Canal is a contour canal and therefore twists this way and that without really getting far. For the inland sailors (and walkers!) it is a leisurely holiday route.

The King's Head

There is a notice on the canal inviting 'captains and galley slaves' to desert their galleys and visit the pub! They will not be disappointed.

Hook Norton beers are served, among them Old Hooky. A favourite for the sailors and walkers here is the Steak Bomb – the meat is heated up with peppers, mushrooms and onions. If this sounds too fiery for you there is always the excellent carvery or something tempting on the specials board. In this friendly pub children and dogs all receive a warm welcome – and there is a garden with plenty of benches and tables. Opening times on Monday to Thursday are 12 noon to 3 pm and 5.30 pm to 11 pm. From Friday to Sunday it is open all day from 12 noon to 11 pm. Telephone: 01926 812202.

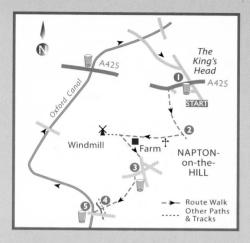

The Walk

① Cross the main road and turn left along the pavement. At a road junction cross back over the road to a signed footpath through a gate. Climb the hill along a hard path. Go through a kissing gate. Keep ahead (left-hand hedge) and through another kissing gate. Maintain the heading to a vehicle way.

② Turn right to walk by the church. Keep ahead at a junction to rest awhile at a viewpoint seat. Here is a rowan tree planted to commemorate the bravery of the Home Guard and Royal Observer Corps during the war. Retrace your steps to the junction and bear right to drop downhill. The way divides – take the right-hand fork to a road.

③ Turn right (Poplar Road) for 100 yards. Climb a stile by a gate on the left. Two paths are signed; take the direction of the right-hand way over the ridge and furrow field. Climb a fence stile in the far right-hand corner. In a paddock field walk alongside a left-hand border to climb a stile to a farm way.

④ Cross to go over a bridge. Walk over a field to a rather hidden stile onto a lane. Turn right and cross the canal.

⑤ Gain the towing path. Continue so the

PLACES OF INTEREST NEARBY

Near the church in Napton-on-the-Hill is **Church Leyes Farm**. This wonderful 40-acre family farm has been run on organic lines way before this became popular. The whole theme is 'in harmony with nature' – the family here recognise they are only guardians of the earth. There is a huge range of interest – the animals, ducks and fowls; forestry (including a saw mill); examples of hedging and so on. The farm is open every day 'except the Judeo Christian Sabbath and other Holy Days'. Telephone 01926 812143.

Looking towards Napton Hill

water is on your right side. The canal twists around bends. After about ¾ mile go under a road bridge then another by a pub. At the next bridge leave the canal. Climb to a lane and turn right. Bear right at a junction to return to the King's Head.

Bishop's Itchington
The Butcher's Arms

MAP: OS LANDRANGER 151 (GR 390579) **WALK 15** **DISTANCE:** 3 MILES

DIRECTIONS TO START: TURN OFF THE A425 ON THE B4452 (5 MILES SOUTH-EAST OF LEAMINGTON SPA) OR THE B4451 (FROM SOUTHAM) AND CONTINUE ALONG THE B4451 TO BISHOP'S ITCHINGTON. THE PUB IS IN FISHER ROAD (OPPOSITE CHURCH CLOSE). **PARKING:** IN THE PUB CAR PARK.

The walk is along the tranquil countryside surrounding the sinuous River Itchen. These were lands belonging to the Bishop of Lichfield. (There were once two settlements – Itchington Superior and Itchington Inferior. Sorry – we stroll from the site of the latter!) Many of the older houses were built to house workers at the local cement works and Greaves (the quarry owner) gave his name to various streets and buildings.

We go along footpaths through woods alive with birdsong and then across arable lands to the main road and a river crossing at Depper's Bridge (built 1939). The road is soon left behind as we continue along quiet lanes for $1/2$ mile. The final section is by a farm where a donkey welcomes visitors, then through arable and pastureland bordering the Itchen back to the village.

The Butcher's Arms

The pub has intense competition in the village – not from other inns but the place is cheek by jowl with two men's clubs. The landlord counters this by offering good homely hospitality to all comers. The beer is well-kept (real ales from Greene King, Ansells and Flowers) and the food is good basic home-cooked traditional fare. The hot bacon baguettes were a welcome snack after a rather damp walk and my vegetarian friend enthused about the cauliflower and broccoli bake with plenty of naughty chips. Children like the playground and Meg my wet dog even received a welcome! The opening hours are 11.30 am to 3 pm and 6 pm to 11 pm on Monday to Saturday and usual times on a Sunday. Telephone: 01926 614161.

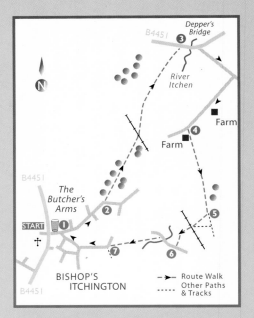

The Walk

① From the car park turn left along the road. At the end of the village and by open countryside the road twists sharp right.

② Keep ahead along a vehicle track which is also a public footpath. Go past houses and under a railway. Follow a wide hedged track – an old green lane no doubt. At a gate enter an arable field. Walk parallel to the right-hand border of the field to a stile onto the B4451.

③ Turn right. Cross over the bridge then turn right at a lane and right again at the next junction. Within ½ mile and as the road bears right take a signed bridleway down the drive of The Folly. (Note – not the drive of Folly Field Farm which was passed earlier.)

④ Walk along the drive and pass a barn. Keep ahead through a gate to a grass paddock where the friendly donkey grazes. Maintain the direction through gates to a coppice. Follow the arrowed direction through the trees and bushes to arable lands. Walk alongside left-hand hedges to a bold waymark post.

⑤ Take the path signed over the open field on the right to a stile in the hedge. (Note – if the field is sown and the path difficult continue to the next field and turn right to the stile.) Climb another stile at a

PLACES OF INTEREST NEARBY

Three miles along lanes to the north-west is a fine **windmill**. Built for Sir Edward Peyto in 1632, Chesterton Mill has been skilfully restored and the sails turn on some summer days. A few miles further north is **Leamington Spa** with its splendid shops, parks and spa buildings.

The welcoming donkey

railway crossing point. Over the tracks turn right then left along a path to a lane.

⑥ Turn right. Cross the river again. At once take a signed path down steps on the left. In the pasture take the arrowed direction with the river now on the left. Walk down the field and through a barrier.

Aim to the left of distant houses and continue to a road.

⑦ Keep ahead (Poplar Road) and ahead at a junction. At a T-junction turn right (Fisher Road) to return to the Butcher's Arms.

Ashorne
The Cottage Tavern

MAP: OS LANDRANGER 151 (GR 303578) **WALK 16** **DISTANCE:** 2½ MILES

DIRECTIONS TO START: ASHORNE IS A MILE EAST OF THE B4087 WELLESBOURNE TO WARWICK ROAD, REACHED ALONG A LANE. THE INN IS ON THE MAIN VILLAGE STREET. **PARKING:** QUIET STREETSIDE.

This is a delightful stroll along quiet tracks and lanes. There are no hills to climb and the countryside is gentle – and even the sheep are friendly! Ashorne was derived from the Anglo-Saxon word for northeast and the hamlet was built in that direction from the old village of Newbold Pacey. There are some lovely cottages where windows peep from under the thatch then we go over arable and sheep lands. The church we pass is at Newbold Pacey and had the same architect (J. Pearson) in 1881 as Truro Cathedral. We then stroll along the borders of what must be one of the most attractively sited cricket fields for many a mile – where you have to cross a little stream to get to and from the pavilion! There are plenty of seats to rest awhile and watch the action.

The Cottage Tavern

This is a pub where you can take it easy – no quick-food establishment but a place to enjoy a leisurely chat whilst your food (not hurriedly removed from a freezer) is cooked. Everything is prepared from fresh ingredients ànd cooked to order within half an hour – and so much better for it. There are wonderful pasta and curry dishes from the menu but watch the board for tempting daily specials. The real ales are Tetley and Morland Old Speckled Hen.

The decor is simple but homely with cricket memorabilia and bar games like darts and billiards, but leave Fido outside – there is a pleasant flower-bedecked patio for him to enjoy. Opening hours are 12 noon to 2.30 pm and 6 pm to 11 pm daily but do phone before to check on times of availability for cooked meals. Telephone: 01926 651410.

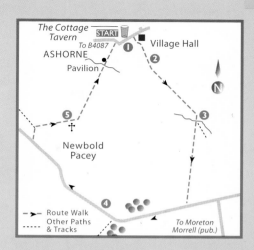

The Walk

① Out of the pub cross the road and turn left along the main street. Within 50 yards take a signed path on the right. Go around the village hall (keep it on your left side) and pass through a gate. Follow the arrowed direction aiming for the right-hand end of a distant row of cupressus trees.

② Pick up the line of an embankment. Keep this on your right side passing an electricity pole with a waymark arrow on it. Go over a corner stile to a large sheep pasture. Gradually leave the left-hand border to walk to the very far right-hand corner of the field.

③ Cross the brook over a railed bridge. There are two paths. Take the right-hand one to maintain the old heading to a stile across the meadow. Walk alongside a right-hand hedge. Continue to a lane. Turn right.

④ Keep on the lane for about a mile. Just after a gas sub-station take a path over a rather concealed stile on the right. Follow the arrowed direction half left to a stile onto a vehicle way. Turn right. Just before the church go through a gate to the left of the church to a sheep pasture.

⑤ Walk alongside a right-hand hedge.

PLACES OF INTEREST NEARBY

Three miles south-west of Ashorne along the B4087 and B4086 is the National Trust's **Charlecote Park**, home to the Lucy family for over 700 years. The splendid house we see today was built in the mid 16th century and Capability Brown did a great job on the garden. The deer (reputedly poached by Shakespeare) seem oblivious to visitors. Open from April to the end of October, Friday to Tuesday. Telephone: 01789 470277.

A sheep pasture at Newbold Pacey

Pass through a corner gate and continue alongside a left-hand hedge. Go over a far broken corner gate and over a brook to the cricket field. Walk along the right-hand border and pass by (not through) a metal kissing gate. Continue to a gate in a brick wall onto a lane. Turn right to the Cottage Tavern.

Lighthorne
The Antelope

MAP: OS LANDRANGER 151 (GR 340558)   **WALK 17**   **DISTANCE:** 1½ MILES

DIRECTIONS TO START: FOLLOW WELL-SIGNED LANES TO LIGHTHORNE OFF THE B4455 (FOSSE WAY) OR THE B4100 SOUTH OF LEAMINGTON SPA. THE ANTELOPE IS IN THE CENTRE OF THE VILLAGE. **PARKING:** THERE IS A CAR PARK BESIDE THE PUB.

The short stroll starts by the little green where there are attractive old thatched cottages. The well where the residents of old collected their water has a Victorian well-head. As we progress westwards, pathways nudge pools where wildfowl gather – these were fish ponds in days past before the age of the fridge!

The return paths skirt a wood and you may get a glimpse of Chesterton Mill on the far side of a noisy motorway. The windmill, on Tuscan pillars designed by Inigo Jones in 1632, has been splendidly renewed and its huge white sails turn on selected days in summertime. The route then continues to Lighthorne's lovely weathered church with its 18th century tower keeping an eye on the village in the hollow. There is some fine glass to be seen here – the windows depict St Lawrence and St Sebastian.

The Antelope

This pub is in a lovely situation high above the little green. Its exact history is somewhat obscure but it is thought to have been here for four hundred years. Lighthorne is a mile or so from any main road so over the centuries this was probably a traditional village hostelry serving mainly agricultural workers. The flags on the floor are a good indication – and are now ideal for ramblers' boots. Today the Antelope depends on its reputation to draw customers from longer distances. How welcoming are the inglenooks with the log fires after a winter walk. In other seasons there is a pleasant garden to enjoy, with benches around the well (which is always filling a bucket!).

A popular dish is the Braised Lamb Shank coated with port and wine sauce and for the vegetarian palate the Jambalaya is highly praised. The puddings include my favourite but naughty Spotted Dick. Real ales on tap are Abbot, Flowers IPA, Wadworth 6X, Marston's Pedigree and always a guest. Meg had to accept the 'No Dogs' rule. The pub is open all day on Saturday and Sunday; during the week the hours are 12 noon to 2.30 pm and 6 pm to 11 pm. Telephone: 01926 651295.

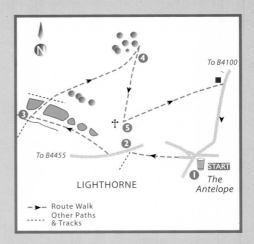

The Walk

① From the pub cross the road and turn right. Within a step or two turn left down a lane signed as a no through road. At the end go along the drive of Rosemary Cottage then follow the arrowed way around a garage to a kissing gate into a pasture. Keep to the right-hand border and around a far bend to the right to pass through a kissing gate onto a lane.

② Turn left. Within 150 yards climb a stile on the right. Cross the meadow to go over another stile. Walk along a winding path over a rough pasture. A series of pools is now passed on the right. Take care going over a dam then keep on the rough path beyond, going by another pool. At the end one path goes left over a brook and stile but we go right.

③ Walk between pools to join a vehicle way. As this bends right keep ahead to go over a stile. Climb the hill, passing just to the left of an elongated wood to a step stile

PLACES OF INTEREST NEARBY

Near Wellesbourne to the south-west is the **Watermill**, which has been lovingly restored. There are guided tours and the long history of the place is described, with grain still ground to produce flour. There is a museum and a fine display of old agricultural implements, a café and shop. Check days and times of opening. Telephone: 01789 470237.

The village well

on the ridgetop. Keep the direction to a stile near the corner of a field that juts into ours. Over the stile gradually leave the left-hand border of the field to continue near a left-hand wood to a double step stile near the far left-hand corner of the field.

④ The route now almost reverses direction. Do not go over the stile. With your back to the stile look half left. Now walk over the sheep pasture to the stile now seen. Keep the direction, aiming just to the left of Lighthorne's church tower.

⑤ Do not pass through the metal gate (unless you are visiting the church) but turn left along the cart track – a bridleway. Follow the track through gates to emerge on a road by a house. Turn right to Lighthorne and the Antelope.

Fenny Compton
The Merrie Lion

MAP: OS LANDRANGER 151 (GR 417524)   **WALK 18**   **DISTANCE:** 3½ MILES

DIRECTIONS TO START: FENNY COMPTON IS 9 MILES NORTH OF BANBURY AND IS REACHED BY TURNING WESTWARDS OFF THE A423 COVENTRY ROAD. THE MERRIE LION IS AT A CROSSROADS IN THE CENTRE OF THE VILLAGE. **PARKING:** IN THE CAR PARK BESIDE THE PUB.

This stroll is from a pretty village of red-hued Hornton stone buildings then along the peaceful towing path of the meandering Oxford Canal. The final mile or so is over the uplands of the Dassett Hills.

Fenny Compton (which means 'a settlement in a marshy vale') has a church, with a short, dumpy spire that overlooks green pastures from its lofty site. The Oxford Canal (which was built over 200 years ago) is a delight to the pleasure boat people today but the despair of the bargees of old. As a contour canal to avoid the necessity of locks the 77-mile waterway twists this way and that – and then is almost at the point where it started!

The Merrie Lion

This is the antithesis of many of today's pubs; it makes no pretence of smart decor or fancy meals but is in the old tradition of country inns, providing basic, welcoming hospitality. My guidebook dated several years ago calls it a 'handsome old inn' – it was built in 1710.

The food tends to be of the 'with chips' variety but is just what you need before or after walking a mile or so on the final high hills of this circuit! Banks's supply the beer although there is always a guest as well. Pub games (as they should be in a traditional inn) are very popular and dogs are allowed if they know their manners. Before you set out on the stroll I hope you are able to check the time (and for Latin scholars the motto 'Ut umbra sic vitae) on the ancient sundial. The pub is open from 12 noon to 3.30 pm and 7 pm to 11 pm on Monday to Saturday and from 12 noon to 3 pm and 7 pm to 10.30 pm on Sunday. In the winter (not the summer as is the norm with other pubs, to 'catch' the tourists) Saturday has all day opening when the local sportsmen are active! Telephone: 01295 770881.

The Walk

① Out of the car park turn left then at once left again to walk along the High Street. Within 300 yards as the road twists sharp right to become Station Road take a signed path on the left. Go through a gap by a metal gate. Within a few steps climb a stile to a field by an estate road. Continue alongside a right-hand hedge.

② After a short distance the path divides; stay by the hedge. Cross a vehicle way over two stiles and keep the old direction. In a far corner go through a gateway then at once go left over a stile. Pass under a railway. Cross a pasture to go under another railway to a stile.

③ Two paths are signed; take the right-hand direction to cross the open field to a hedge. Turn right alongside the hedge. Follow this to a stile as you are nearing a road. Continue to a white painted gate onto the road.

④ Cross to the path signed opposite. Go along the vehicle way to the marina. Nearing the canal veer to the left to pass the canalside chandlery (well-stocked shop). With the water on your left walk along the towing path for about ¾ mile. Cross the canal over an elegant wrought-iron bridge just before a high modern bridge. At once leave the waterway and follow a path to the road.

⑤ Turn right to cross the canal and the railway. Immediately take a signed bridleway right. In the field go left to pick up a bold tractor way that cuts across the field to a far wide hedge gap. Keep the heading with a hedge on your left. Ignore other signed paths and keep on the tractor way to emerge on a narrow lane near a barn.

PLACES OF INTEREST NEARBY

Two miles to the west of Fenny Compton are the **Burton Dassett Hills**. This country park (once the source of iron ore) is the place to fly kites and for children to chase and play. A deserted village is sited here but all that remains is a wonderful church – the 'Cathedral of the Hills'.

The marina at Fenny Compton

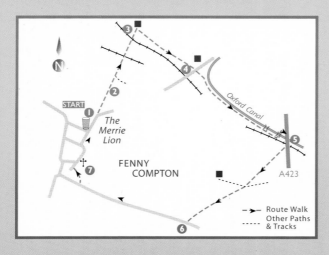

⑥ Turn right. Within about a mile and opposite a farmstead called The Grange go over a stile on the right.

⑦ In the pasture make for a point just to the left of the church. Go through a gate to Dog Lane. Turn right then right again at a road. Opposite the war memorial turn right – the High Street goes back to the Merrie Lion.

Welford-on-Avon
The Bell Inn

| MAP: OS LANDRANGER 151 (GR 148522) | **WALK 19** | DISTANCE: 3 MILES |

DIRECTIONS TO START: WELFORD-ON-AVON IS 4 MILES WEST OF STRATFORD-ON-AVON ALONG THE B439. TURN SOUTHWARDS ALONG A SIGNED LANE. THE BELL INN IS BY THE LITTLE GREEN IN THE CENTRE OF THE VILLAGE. **PARKING:** THERE IS A CAR PARK AT THE SIDE OF THE PUB.

The stroll starts along a lane which is often photographed – here are the cottages capped by thatch under which the 'eye' windows peep and where the roses climb over the doorways. Nearby is the church (established by the monks of Deerhurst in Saxon times), much of which the Normans knew. Then we amble beside the Avon – a rushing torrent at first by the mill weir then tranquil and reeded. Coming back into the village we encounter a wonderful indication of the quirkiness of the English – a striped maypole that at 65 ft tops everything around. A second village (Weston-on-Avon) is visited; the church of All Saints has been looking across the river since the 15th century. The return path nudges another stretch of the Avon.

The Bell Inn

I remember the Bell Inn thirty or so years ago when one could get a good curry here – many years before the advent of universal pub food and when crisps and a cheese sandwich was the standard fare elsewhere. The good curries are still obtainable but the choice of food here is now much wider. The Beaujolais Beef (with red wine, herbs and prunes) would be a fine reward for completing the walk but the snacks such as Avocado and Smoked Bacon Salad are a feast in themselves.

Old prints show that the exterior of the Bell has little changed in a hundred years; inside is another story – the welcoming ambience created by beamed ceilings (carrying succinct mottoes like 'A quart of ale is a dish for a king'), polished brass and wintertime log fires is delightfully merged with modern comfortable furnishings. There is a choice of many real ales including Wadworth 6X, Boddingtons, Hobsons and Flowers and always a guest beer. The times of opening are 11.30 am to 3.30 pm and 6 pm to 11 pm on Monday to Saturday and 12 noon to 4 pm and 7 pm to 11 pm on Sunday. Telephone: 01789 750353.

The Walk

① From the car park turn right then at once right again (Church Street) at the little green. The road passes those lovely cottages (with names such as 'Ten Penny' and 'The Owl Pen') and the church. (Note the 14th century lychgate and site of the pound and stocks.)

② At the end take the path left. At a

The lofty maypole at Welford

vehicle way go left then immediately right to enter a little caravan site. Follow the vehicle way to a stile onto a footpath which runs near the right-hand river. After about ⅓ mile climb a stile. Just beyond climb steps left to a lane.

③ Turn left. At the bottom of the hill is a T-junction.

PLACES OF INTEREST NEARBY

Eight miles south-west along the B439 and B4085 is one of the largest tithe barns in the country at **Middle Littleton**. Under the care of the National Trust it dates from the 13th century and is still used as a farm building. Open from April to November inclusive.

Welford-on-Avon

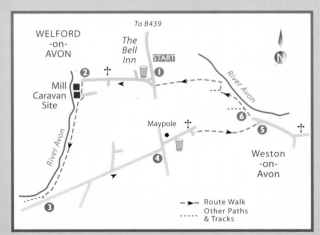

houses and over arable fields to a vehicle way. Continue to a lane by a waymark post.

⑤ Turn right to the church at Weston-on-Avon then retrace your steps to the waymark post. Follow the direction of the signed bridleway (blue arrow) to pass in front of houses. Drop down to the river. The path divides; take the right-hand arrowed way.

⑥ At a vehicle way walk for 20 yards then take a signed path right. At another vehicle way go right then at once keep ahead along a signed path as the vehicle way sweeps right. Look for a waymark by a rough pasture to take us right. The path then borders the left-hand rough pasture and leads to a road near the Bell Inn.

④ Turn left and right (Chapel Street) by the maypole (erected in 1967). The spreading chestnut tree commemorated the Silver Jubilee of 1935. Within 300 yards take a signed path down Pool Close to the right. Immediately leave the road by bearing left along a footpath. Keep ahead past

Clifford Chambers
The New Inn

MAP: OS LANDRANGER 151 (GR 194525) · **WALK 20** · **DISTANCE:** 3½ MILES

DIRECTIONS TO START: CLIFFORD CHAMBERS IS REACHED ON THE B4632 SOUTH OF STRATFORD-UPON AVON. THE PUB IS BY THE JUNCTION WITH THE MAIN VILLAGE STREET. **PARKING:** IN THE LARGE CAR PARK IN FRONT OF THE PUB.

Clifford Chambers is in a quiet lane that leads to nowhere but how different it might have been! Some aver that Shakespeare was not born at Stratford but in this little village. The theory goes that the plague had come to the town so his mother 'escaped' to the village for the birth. Proof there is none so fortunately the gaping crowds leave Clifford Chambers to us. There are several fine ancient buildings here including the 17th century Manor House (mainly rebuilt by Lutyens) and the gabled timbered rectory (where a John Shakespeare lived). The Norman masons have left their distinctive mark in the church and we can also marvel at the Jacobean pulpit.

The stroll is a delicious mixture of fieldpaths and lanes and passes by the hamlet of Atherstone on Stour where the church only dates from 1876. A few years ago it was declared unsafe; I will not embarrass anyone by naming the builder – who perhaps is now learning a thing or two from the Normans in the Elysian Fields!

The New Inn

I was told this was a coaching inn; I was not (quite) around at that time to verify this but I have my doubts! The village was not on a main turnpike route and the place is more likely to have supplied the wants of the farming community. However, the 'new' aspect seems to indicate that the present building where roses climb to the eaves may have replaced an earlier 15th century hostelry.

Bass is the real ale served and there is an extensive menu both for the restaurant and bar snacks. I loved the Chicken Satay 'served with a spicy peanut sauce' and the veggie dish 'topped with a walnut and cheddar crumble' looked good. There are plenty of tables and benches outside for those warmer days and you can stay longer in one of the twelve bed and breakfast rooms. The pub is open from 12 noon to 3 pm and 6 pm to 11 pm on Monday to Friday and all day on Saturday and Sunday. Telephone: 01789 293402.

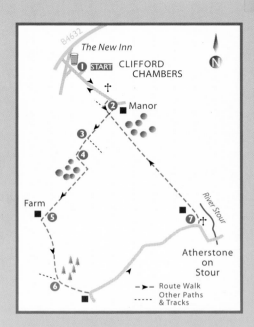

The Walk

① From the car park turn left to walk down the main street (signed as a no through road) to pass the Rectory and church. Nearing the Manor House look for a signed footpath on the right.

② Within a few steps there is a T-junction of paths. Turn left to a farm road. Turn right.

③ When the farm road divides take the right-hand way. After a yard or two swing left. The path is alongside a right-hand hedge and climbs gently towards woodland.

④ At the woods turn 90 degrees left (trees on the right) then right at the corner. Continue beside the right-hand woodland. Pass through a corner gap of the field and now walk by a left-hand hedge. Go through a hedge gap and regain the old heading (hedge now on the right).

PLACES OF INTEREST NEARBY

Preston on Stour (4 miles south) is a typical 'estate' village. Many of the houses were built in Tudor style in the middle of the 19th century. The 'big house' (not open to the public) is Alscot Park. It is still the home of the West family and was bought by James West in 1749. Just east of Clifford Chambers along the B4632 is the **Shire Horse Centre**. Open daily (restrictions in winter) there are many animals besides the horses and many attractions for children including a 'Country Village Experience'. Telephone: 01789 415274.

The old rectory

⑤ Drop down to climb a stile by a metal gate beside barns. Turn left to continue by a left-hand hedge to climb a far corner stile. On the same heading strike out over the open field, aiming for the right-hand corner of a wood.

⑥ Climb a stile to a rough farm track. Turn left. Follow the wide track to twist left by a house to a lane. Keep ahead to drop down to Atherstone on Stour. Pass the huge old rectory (note the 15 windows at the front!).

⑦ As the lane twists sharp right near the old church building take a signed path along a farm road on the left. When the road bends to the left to a barn keep ahead along the footpath beside a wire fence. Maintain the heading to the farm road where we were earlier. Cross to the stile and retrace your steps to the New Inn.

Ettington
The White Horse

MAP: OS LANDRANGER 151 (GR 272487)   **WALK 21**   **DISTANCE:** 3½ MILES

DIRECTIONS TO START: ETTINGTON IS 6 MILES FROM STRATFORD-UPON-AVON ON THE A422 BANBURY ROAD. THE WHITE HORSE INN IS ON THE SOUTH EDGE OF THE VILLAGE.
PARKING: IN FRONT OF THE PUB.

Ettington is an ancient village well known to travellers of old as here two major coaching highways crossed – we go by one of the tollhouses. The main settlement was once some mile and a half distant. In 1778 the Shirleys (said to be the oldest family in the kingdom) landscaped their garden and wanted peace and quiet. They built a 'new' church for the 'other' folk; today the lovely old church with its work of the Norman masons nudges rather uncomfortably the 19th century Hall which is now an exclusive country hotel. The 'new' church which we pass on this stroll was built of cheap inferior stone and lasted only a hundred years with just the truncated tower left to tell the story.

This stroll takes us over some splendid open countryside and alongside woods where the birds never seem to stop their serenading.

The White Horse

This is a pub that is not afraid to advertise its attractions, particularly its warm welcome and 'the atmosphere of days gone by' – how true. There is a lounge but I love the 'Juggery' where 299 jugs line the beams! There are often 'theme' evenings and Tuesday is always fresh fish night with a special delivery from Grimsby. Marston's Pedigree and Fuller's London Pride are the favourite real ales. There is a pretty orchard garden for those days of summer sun. The White Horse is open from 12 noon to 2.30 pm and 6.30 pm to 11 pm on Monday to Saturday; normal Sunday hours apply. There are also four en suite rooms for overnight accommodation. Telephone: 01789 740641.

The Walk

① From the car park turn left along the main road to the roundabout. Turn left (A429) for a few steps then cross the road. A footpath sign directs us up the embankment.

② Go over a stile to a farm drive. Turn left. Walk past the farmhouse (on the left). At barns follow the waymarked route to the right of the barns then by left-hand silos.

③ Go past new barns then take a path bearing half left over the open field. Aim for the right-hand end of a wood.

④ At the wood bear left to continue at the border of the woodland and the field. Climb a stile and stay by the trees. At the far corner go a few yards right then left to regain the old heading.

⑤ Walk alongside a right-hand hedge. When the hedge ends veer slightly right over an open field to a stile in the hedge. Turn left on the lane.

⑥ After about 250 yards climb a stile on the left. In the field follow the arrowed way, aiming just to the left of a distant house with tall chimneys. Go through a wide hedge gap and keep the same heading in the next field to a stile leading to a pasture.

⑦ Bear right and proceed to the far right hand corner. Climb a stile and bear right past a solitary oak to a metal gate. Climb the embankment to a main road.

⑧ Cross to the signed path almost opposite. Continue to a stile with a pasture beyond. Take the arrowed direction. Cross a farm vehicle way (barn on the right) and go to a stile onto a lane by a five-bar gate.

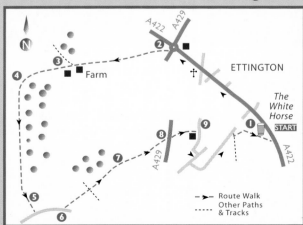

ETTINGTON

The White Horse

START

Farm

— ►— Route Walk
Other Paths
----- & Tracks

The old church lasted only a hundred years

⑨ Turn right. At a T-junction turn right then at once left (Roger's Lane). Just past a layby (on the left) look for a post on the right with two paths signed. Take the left-hand way. Go left around a field to a far hedge gap. A hedged way leads to a road and the A422. The White Horse is to the left.

PLACES OF INTEREST NEARBY
Wellesbourne Watermill is a mile south of Wellesbourne on the B4086 (see Walk 17). Ettington is only 6 miles from Stratford-upon-Avon, north along the A422. Here almost everything is 'Shakespeare' but there are fascinating riverside paths and walks – feeding the swans is a popular pastime.

Ratley
The Rose and Crown

DIRECTIONS TO START: RATLEY IS 8 MILES NORTH-WEST OF BANBURY, JUST OFF THE B4086. THE PUB IS AT THE END OF A CUL-DE-SAC LANE NEAR THE CHURCH. **PARKING:** ON THE QUIET ROAD OUTSIDE THE PUB.

Ratley is built with the local ruddy-hued ironstone from Hornton quarries – a warm stone this which gives an instant cosy feeling that is reflected in this quiet 'away from it all' Warwickshire village on steep streets. The branch railway which should have come to carry the stone to the main line at Fenny Compton was never completed – the cutting is there up Edgehill but an accident in 1913 stopped the work.

On this stroll we go near the weatherworn church which has a rare dedication to St Peter ad Vincula. There is a hoary old cross in the churchyard but look at the war memorial. Some say this is the inspiration for 'There'll always be an England' with seventeen Englands going to the First World War and four not returning.

Within the parish boundary (and seen in the distance from this walk), is Edgehill – the great Civil War battle of 1642 was fought below the steep escarpment. On the other side of a vale we see the site of a Bronze Age settlement which covered 17 acres.

The Rose and Crown

The Rose and Crown was built in 1098 as a cottage to house the stonemasons working on the church. Later, as an inn, it served travellers on the main Banbury to Stratford highway before a new road was constructed. It exudes history, which is heightened when the Sealed Knot Society come to re-enact the great Civil War fight. The inglenooks in this free house selling Wells' real ales are huge and there are solid beams – and the flagstones on the floor can cope with walkers' boots. It was only a few decades ago that the beer ceased coming in jugs through the serving hatch. Dogs, like strollers, are given a warm welcome as also it would seem is the Roundhead ghost.

The menu is not huge but will satisfy all tastes. The baguettes particularly are crammed full. The pub is open on Monday to Friday from noon to 2.30 pm and 6 pm to 11 pm. On Saturdays and Sundays there is all day opening from 12 noon. Telephone: 01295 678148.

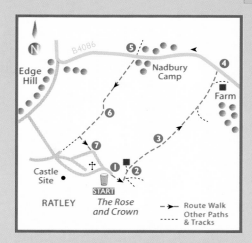

The Walk

① Out of the pub turn right along the lane. Soon the lane becomes a steeply climbing farm drive. As the drive bears sharp left to a house, climb a stile. Two paths are signed. Take the left-hand path to follow a way beside the drive to a corner stile.

② Continue (house on left) to another corner stile by a metal gate. Keep the same heading alongside a left-hand hedge. On the hill we see Nadbury Camp on the opposite ridge. Drop down to a rather concealed corner stile. Beyond, the path follows a way a few yards to the right of the left-hand border of the field. Make for a spot under a far rowan tree about 50 yards to the right of a corner.

③ Go through a wide hedge gap and climb the hill. Go over a corner fence stile and maintain the heading to join a vehicle drive. Pass through a gate. As the vehicle way sweeps right to a house keep ahead to climb a stile. Continue to a road (the B4086).

④ Turn left. On a bend we can see the Civil War battle site in the vale (now covered by an armaments dump).

⑤ After ¾ mile of road walking look for a signed path through bushes on the left. Take the arrowed way descending across an open field. Drop down to a bridge then take the indicated route climbing a gentle rise. Go through a distant corner hedge gap and follow a clear path beyond.

⑥ Border a left-hand hedge for 50 yards then bear half right over the open field. On the ridge make for the middle of a row of

The ancient village inn

cupressus trees to the left of a house. Pick up a hidden left-hand stone wall to a stone stile on the left. Go across the rough hill pasture to join a fence by a house. Follow the path to a lane.

⑦ Turn left to the Rose and Crown, taking time to look at the church on your way back to the pub.

PLACES OF INTEREST NEARBY

Two miles along lanes to the south-west of Ratley is the National Trust's **Upton House**. The mansion was built in 1695 and has fine grounds – the water garden is particularly interesting. Inside are rare paintings, tapestries and furniture. Open daily April to November except Thursday and Friday. Telephone: 01295 670266.

Halford
The Halford Bridge Inn

MAP: OS LANDRANGER 151 (GR 261455)   **WALK 23**   **DISTANCE:** 3½ MILES

DIRECTIONS TO START: HALFORD IS ON THE FOSSE WAY (A429) 8 MILES SOUTH-EAST OF STRATFORD-UPON-AVON. THE BELL INN IS JUST NORTH OF THE BRIDGE OVER THE RIVER STOUR. **PARKING:** THERE IS A CAR PARK IN FRONT OF THE PUB.

For much of this ramble we are above the lovely valley of the meandering River Stour. This is pastoral country and the cattle mutely stare as though surprised to see us folk, like them, appreciating their territory. Most of Halford is secretly cosseted off the main road which must have been much quieter when the Roman legions tramped this way. The village has lost its school (now the village hall) but the church treasures much from the time of the Normans and a bell in the 13th century tower has been calling worshippers for almost five hundred years.

The pub overlooks the historic stone bridge (now pensioned off) where the Royalists lost a battle during the Civil War. On the other side of the race-track road is a 200-year-old bowling club, once an exclusive gathering of men of standing like the Sanderson Millers, the Verneys and Leighs.

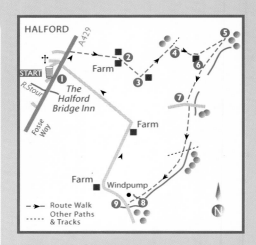

The Halford Bridge Inn

This was the Bell until recently but as there are several other 'Bells' in the area the change is understandable. The pub is a classic Georgian building dating from 1576 and the blocked archway gives the clue that this was once an important coaching inn on the Fosse Way.

This privately owned pub has a homely feel especially when there are open log fires in wintertime. Besides the Fosse Way Bar and beamed restaurant there is a pleasant courtyard area. En suite overnight accommodation is available and the chef has a fine reputation locally. Although there are such delicacies as whole smoked trout, herrings in madeira sauce and game, I can recommend for ramblers the home-made pies – try the chicken and mushroom! The beers are Bass and a guest ale. The pub is open all day on Saturdays and Sundays but on other days the hours are 11 am to 2.30 pm and 6 pm to 11 pm. Telephone: 01789 740382.

The Walk

① From the car park cross the main road and turn left. Within 400 yards turn right down the drive of Molesman Farm which is signed as a footpath. The drive is straight to the farm. Walk to the right of the buildings and look for yellow waymark arrows.

② Past a cottage swing left then at once turn right so regaining the old heading. As you walk along a vehicle way there is now a new galvanized barn on the left. Go over a stile adjoining a gate.

③ At a junction of vehicle ways by a large house turn left. Pass through a gate and keep ahead. The tarmac way becomes a wide stony track.

④ By a wood (on the left) the way divides. Take the way going right towards an old barn. Walk around the barn (easier to the left). Just past the barn bear left over the open field so leaving the main track. Make for the far left corner of an elongated wood.

⑤ At the wood turn almost back on yourself – nearly reversing the old heading over the open field. Make for the right hand corner of another wood. Reaching the corner keep ahead (with the wood and a wooden fence on the left).

⑥ Pass through a metal gate. Keep ahead alongside a right-hand hedge. Pass through a corner gate and maintain the direction in the next field to a lane.

PLACES OF INTEREST NEARBY
Seven miles north of Halford along the A429 then the B4086 is **Charlecote Park** (see Walk 16).

Halford

⑦ Cross over through the opposite gate. Follow an undefined way alongside the left hand brook to pass through a far corner metal gate. Still keep near the left-hand brook. Go through a distant gate then along a rough track alongside right-hand woods.

⑧ At the end of the woods enter a pasture. Bear right, aiming to the left of a windpump. Pass through a metal gate to a lane.

⑨ Turn right to climb the hill and keep to the lane (bearing left at a junction by a farm) to Halford.

Ilmington
The Howard Arms

MAP: OS LANDRANGER 151 (GR 213437)   **WALK 24**   **DISTANCE:** 2½ MILES

DIRECTIONS TO START: ILMINGTON IS 8 MILES SOUTH OF STRATFORD-UPON-AVON. TURN OFF THE A3400 OR THE A429 ALONG SIGNPOSTED LANES. THE PUB WILL BE FOUND IN THE CENTRE OF THE VILLAGE ON THE LOWER GREEN. **PARKING:** IN FRONT OF THE PUB OR IN THE CAR PARK AT THE REAR.

Ilmington does not suffer from being known as one of the prettiest villages in Warwickshire. It is a scattered community and the lucky residents love to share the beauty with visitors. In April up to ten gardens including the Manor are open to the public and if the day is fine up to a thousand people will come and say 'Oh how beautiful'.

The charm of the village can be so irresistible that the walk may well be delayed a little. Do visit the Norman church and hunt the eleven carved mice on the furnishings. A recently completed tapestry apple map hangs on the north wall. Then there is the old pound – and beware, there are plans to restore the village stocks! Ilmington has the last remaining traditional Morris dancers in the county and they regularly perform in the gardens and outside the Howard Arms. There is a fine network of pathways and lanes around this heavenly village, and on this stroll we explore to the south.

The Howard Arms

The Cotswold stone pub dating from around 1610 overlooks the chestnut-tree-bedecked lower village green. It is rather upmarket but welcomes ramblers – the flagged floor in the bar is boot-proof. The Howard is a favourite haunt for thespians from nearby Stratford so you may well recognise a face or two.

The Bill of Fare is chalked on a huge board on the wall; there is a very wide range of dishes. The salmon is especially good and the inevitable meat pie is deliciously different – perhaps flavoured with beer or Guinness! A selection of real ale includes Flowers and John Smith's and guests. Opening hours are 11 am to 3 pm and 7 pm to 11 pm on Monday to Saturday with the usual Sunday times. Telephone: 01608 682226.

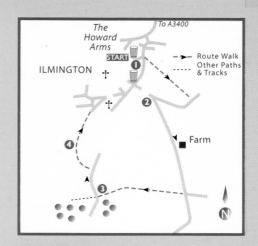

The Walk

① Leaving the pub go over the little green. Walk up the slope to the left of cottages. Go over a stile and follow the clear path to a stile on the crest of the hill. Keep the same direction, now gradually descending to a road. Turn right for 300 yards.

The manor fish pond at Ilmington

② At a junction turn left (signed for Compton Scorpion). Follow the lane past a farm. At a meeting of lanes turn right along a bridleway between arable land. This is an old drovers' road called Pig Lane. Go through a gate and maintain the direction alongside left-hand borders of fields. Climb to the top of the ridge (steep climb).

③ At a lane turn right. Within 200 yards climb a stile on the left (note the old obsolete stone stile alongside). Cross the field to the opposite stile to the locally-known 'humpty-dumpty' pasture. Here were the quarries which provided the limestone from which many of Ilmington's houses were built.

④ Go down the gully which gradually curves to the right to a stile by a gate. Still descending, go along a wide green track which becomes Grump Street and leads back to the village and the Howard Arms.

PLACES OF INTEREST NEARBY
Just over the border and into Gloucestershire from Ilmington is the National Trust's **Hidcote Manor Garden**. Phone 01386 438333 for times of opening.

Tredington
The White Lion

DIRECTIONS TO START: TREDINGTON IS 8 MILES SOUTH OF STRATFORD-UPON-AVON ALONG THE A3400. THE PUB IS ON THE RIGHT IF ENTERING THE VILLAGE FROM THE NORTH. **PARKING:** IN THE CAR PARK AT THE SIDE OF THE PUB.

This is a walk for a day when strolling along fieldpaths elsewhere may be 'soggy' as the route only takes in one footpath and even that can be avoided by keeping to lovely, narrow, squeezed lanes where few motors venture.

The treasure of Tredington (which was the village of the Saxon Tyrdda) is its church with a splendid, tall 15th century spire which is a landmark for miles and where the door has been swinging on its hinges for almost 500 years. We can see the bullet marks from the Civil War but have to take someone's word that there are seven bullets still embedded!

Nearby are cottages topped by thatch; the roses climb high to the eaves – these are the places which sad exiles in far off lands wistfully sigh for. Not long ago they would have been humble dwellings – now each is a sought after 'des.res.'. There were once two starch factories in the village and these together with the mill (now a private house) employed many of the cottagers.

The White Lion

This pub was once an important hotel on the main stage route to Oxford. Much of the building is from the 16th century and stables and a farrier's forge were attached. This is a traditional English pub – nothing pretentious but full of cosiness and charm – you know the sort of thing – low beams, polished brass and local folk. Visit in summertime and you may be entertained by the Ilmington Morrismen who call regularly. There are plenty of benches and tables on the back lawn – pity about the main road traffic noise though.

Food is traditional pub fare but if you qualify do visit for a senior citizen lunch – wonderful value. The real ale is Wadworth 6X and there is always a guest beer available. The daily opening hours are 11.30 am to 3 pm and 6 pm to 11 pm. Telephone: 01608 661522.

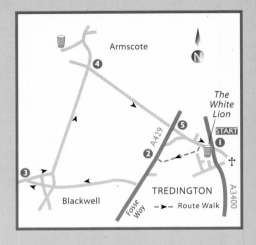

The Walk

① From the car park turn left along the main road. Within a few steps turn left (Armscote Road). After 200 yards take a signed path on the left. Follow the path to an estate road. Turn left then at once right. At the end of the cul-de-sac there is a

One of the charming thatched cottages in Tredington

rather overgrown path (it clears after about 40 yards). In a field follow the left-hand border (which soon turns a corner) to a stile onto the A429 – the Romans' Fosse Way. Note: if the fields are wet it is advisable to follow the lane to the A429 as indicated on the map.

② Turn left. After 300 yards cross the road to take the lane signed to Blackwell. At a crossroads keep ahead (signed to Ilmington). At the next crossroads (by Blackwell Fuchsias) keep ahead. Within a few yards is the centre of the hamlet.

③ Turn right at a T-junction. At the next meeting of lanes bear left (signed to Armscote). The name plaque for Armscote

is reached. (Note: there is another fine pub – the Fox and Goose – in Armscote.)

④ Turn right (signed to Tredington). The lane goes to the Fosse Way. Cross and turn right.

⑤ Within a few yards turn left. Armscote Road leads back to the White Lion.

PLACES OF INTEREST NEARBY

Chipping Campden is 8 miles south-west along the A429 and B4035. This is a famous Cotswold Wool town with a magnificent 'wool' church (120 ft high tower). The mile-long High Street was laid out in the 12th century and contains the National Trust Market Hall given to the town by Sir Baptist Hicks in 1627.

Brailes
The Gate Inn

MAP: OS LANDRANGER 151 (GR 305400)   **WALK 26**   **DISTANCE:** 2½ MILES

DIRECTIONS TO START: BRAILES IS ON THE B4035 ROAD BETWEEN SHIPSTON-ON-STOUR AND BANBURY. THE PUB IS ON THE MAIN ROAD AT UPPER BRAILES. **PARKING:** ROADSIDE.

The walk takes in much of interest in this extensive village and its environs. This was once one of the biggest market towns in the county with the wealth centred on sheep. The large church reflects this past history and has been termed the 'Cathedral of the Feldon' (the southern agricultural part of Warwickshire as opposed to the northern Forest of Arden). We pass an old village pump then reach the splendid man-made mound on which a castle was perched.

We continue through ridge and furrow fields to the Catholic church in Lower Brailes. This humble place of worship was constructed in the upper part of a barn. The church was given to the Augustinians but after the Reformation came to the Bishop family. They opened the church to the public in 1726.

Then the route takes us to the 'Cathedral' church. This goes along and up the 99 steps – do count them as I have got some doubts as to the authenticity of the number!

The Gate Inn

Little is known about the history of this pub – but it is more likely to have satisfied the local farm worker rather than the sophisticated needs of the traveller of days gone by. The style is hospitable simplicity. There are no fancy meals offered on the chalked board and everyone talked about the home-made steak and kidney pie and the local trout. The decor in the two bars is homely – open fireplaces, a welcome for dogs, horse brasses over the inglenook and on the beams.

This is a Hook Norton pub with the local brew joined each week by a different guest beer. The Gate is open all day on Saturday and Sunday. During the week the hours are 11 am to 2.30 pm and 6 pm to 11 pm but note there are no meals on Mondays. Telephone: 01608 685212.

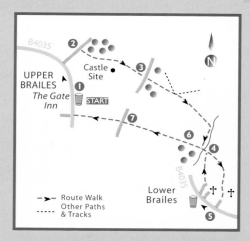

The Walk

① Out of the pub turn right along the B4035. Go right (Castle Hill) at a junction by the old village pump.

② Within 200 yards take a signed path between houses on the right. Climb a stile and keep ahead to a metal gate. Two paths are signed here; take the left-hand path to walk to the left of the castle mound. Climb a fence stile and keep ahead to a stile onto a lane.

③ Cross to the opposite path to a ridge and furrow field (one of the many surrounding the village). Take the arrowed direction. At a far stile two paths are signed; take the right-hand way numbered 52f over the open field. Climb a stile to a rough pasture. Turn right to follow a left hand brook to a bridge.

④ Go over the water. Keep ahead over the

The path to Castle Hill

Castle Hill, Brailes

open pasture (path numbered 52). Over a stile bear right to follow near a right-hand churchyard to a corner stile. Go into the car park of the Catholic church. Turn right then continue along Friars Lane to the B4035.

⑤ Turn right past the way to the church. At the next junction and opposite the George turn right along Butcher's Lane. Follow the vehicle way to a stile on the left. In the pasture take the arrowed direction. Make for the right-hand corner of a distant wood to reach the bridge where we were previously.

⑥ Over the water keep ahead up the 99 steps with woods on the left. Climb the

bank. Follow the path over the open field. There is a division of ways – still keep the old heading to a stile to a lane.

⑦ Cross to the opposite path and maintain the direction to a kissing gate to the main road. Turn right to the pub.

PLACES OF INTEREST NEARBY

Along lanes to the north of Brailes is the beautifully restored **windmill** that catches the wind on a hill near Upper Tysoe. Nearby is the Tudor mansion of **Compton Wynyates**, the seat of the Marquis of Northampton. Although it has been called 'the most perfect house of its age in England' it has to be admired from afar as it is not open to the public.

Shipston-on-Stour
The Coach and Horses

MAP: OS LANDRANGER 151 (GR 259405)   **WALK 27**   **DISTANCE:** 2 MILES

DIRECTIONS TO START: SHIPSTON IS 10 MILES SOUTH OF STRATFORD-UPON-AVON ALONG THE A3400. THE PUB IS ON THE A3400 JUST SOUTH OF THE CENTRE OF THE TOWN. **PARKING:** THERE IS A SMALL PUB CAR PARK BUT THE FREE PUBLIC CAR PARK IS NEAR THE BRIDGE OVER THE STOUR.

Shipston is one of those old-fashioned towns that we thought did not survive in today's world. There are no large supermarkets but a proliferation of little shops including two butchers. From the name you may guess that this was a wool town – correct! There are elegant buildings of the Georgian period but Shipston never enjoyed the wealth of typical Cotswold places (although some say it had 'one of the greatest sheep markets in the kingdom') so the church is charming but humble, rebuilt in the 19th century by the celebrated G. E. Street. The abrupt tower has been looking over the town for 500 years. Feudal Shipston rather went to sleep until the arrival of the stagecoach traffic which spawned many coaching inns.

On the walk we pass through Barcheston where there is a church with a Pisa-like 14th century leaning tower. After the Enclosure Act and an outbreak of cholera the village lost almost all its inhabitants so today we find only a handful of farmsteads. However, there was one famous son – William Sheldon set up his looms here to bring tapestry weaving to England in 1561.

The Coach and Horses

This is an unpretentious but homely pub that is gay with flowers in summertime and sports a patio where the local game Aunt Sally is played. Dating from the early 19th century the inn was one of those important places that provided shelter and refreshments to the stage-coach travellers. We are reminded of past days by the attractive inn sign.

The food served here is a delicious mixture of traditional in the bar and more up-market in the restaurant. Try the traditional steak and kidney pie or the fish and chips or the more pricey oven-baked chicken supreme and you will welcome the exercise to walk it off . . . or you can stay the night – there are four en suite rooms. The ales to tickle your palate include the full range of the local Hook Norton beers. The opening hours are 12 noon to 3 pm and 6 pm to 11 pm on Monday to Thursday; open all day on Friday, Saturday and Sunday. Telephone: 01608 661335.

The Walk

① From the pub cross the road and turn left. Follow the road (now the B4035 Brailes road) around to the right to cross the river over the 18th century bridge. (The building nearby was a flour mill – today it is a rather attractive restaurant.)

② Within 200 yards climb a stile to a pasture on the right. Follow the borders of fields (with the river on the right) with a series of stiles to emerge at the end of a cul-de-sac lane at Barcheston.

③ Turn left for about 50 yards then take a signed footpath to the right. Now in arable

Barcheston church

The Manor House, Shipston-on-Stour

lands follow the clear path to a signposted junction just before the hamlet of Willington.

④ Turn right along a bridleway which crosses over the river. Follow the clear track to the A3400. Turn right to Shipston-on-Stour. The A3400 is quite a busy road but there is a pavement.

PLACES OF INTEREST NEARBY

The **Wellington Aviation Museum** at Moreton-in-Marsh (7 miles south-west along the A429) is of interest both to aeroplane enthusiasts and everyone else. It contains fascinating items of national and local aviation and is described as 'a collection of Royal Air Force jewels'. Open every day except Monday from 10 am to 5 pm. Telephone: 01608 650323.

Stretton-on-Fosse
The Plough Inn

MAP: OS LANDRANGER 151 (GR 222385)   **WALK 28**   **DISTANCE:** 2½ MILES

DIRECTIONS TO START: STRETTON-ON-FOSSE IS JUST OFF THE A429 (FOSSE WAY) 4 MILES NORTH OF MORETON-IN-MARSH. THE PUB IS AT THE CROSSROADS IN THE CENTRE OF THE VILLAGE. **PARKING:** IN THE CAR PARK IN FRONT OF THE PUB.

Hurrah for postcodes – besides many other Strettons throughout the kingdom there are three in Warwickshire! The great Roman highway just nudges Stretton-on-Fosse but there is little evidence of their occupation. Saxon excavations have been made hereabouts and interesting relics of the period found. If evidence of the revered position of the village rector in past days is required just examine the respective sizes of the church and the huge rectory that was built in 1690. Lovers of Victorian architecture enthuse about the little parish church of Saint Peter but this was rebuilt in 1841 so perhaps the earlier building was grander.

The village is a nice mixture of old and new where cottages of thatch rub eaves with new developments – sad that the shop and school have long gone. Announcements of events are made on a huge tree trunk by Old Tree Cottages.

The walk starts over sheep pastures then follows an upland ridge where the views are wonderful. The return to Stretton is along a quiet lane.

The Plough Inn

I remember this pub a few years ago when one wondered if it would survive. The Plough became a free house and has been rejuvenated. It is away from any major road and therefore (in a small village) is dependent on reputation and word of mouth to attract customers – and it succeeds.

The meals in the small cosy bars and restaurant are excellent with a frequently changing menu. There are old favourites with especially good steaks but if you are a 'golden oldie' try one of their bargain lunches – such good value. In wintertime there are spit roasts on the lounge open fire. The selection of beers includes Ansells and Tetley bitters. With Monday closing the Plough is open six days a week (but seven in summer) from 12 noon to 2.30 pm and 6 pm to 11 pm. Telephone: 01608 661053.

The Walk

① From the car park turn right to walk along the village street. Pass the village hall (built in 1998). Within 400 yards the great tree is reached.

② The main street bears sharp right; maintain the old heading along a short cul-de-sac, passing the sign 'Old Tree Cottages'. Climb a stile beside a metal gate. Take the arrowed direction over a pasture. Climb another stile in the opposite fence. Maintain the heading over sheep pastures. (Glance back for a view of the Old Rectory.) Aim for distant road signs on the main road just to the right of an elongated wood.

PLACES OF INTEREST NEARBY

About 5 miles south-west of Stretton-on-Fosse is the **Batsford Arboretum and Falconry Centre**. It is in the grounds of the splendid Batsford Park which was the seat of the Redesdale family. The Centre is open daily. Telephone: 01386 701441.

③ Climb a stile to the A429. At once turn right down a lane to pass a seat. At a road junction by a little green keep ahead as the main road bears right. Pass between pillars. Go between more pillars (there is a large house with a fine sundial nearby).

④ At once swing left along a vehicle way. Go past barns and through a metal gate.

Stretton-on-Fosse Manor House

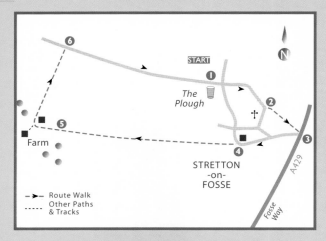

⑤ Go through a corner hunting gate. (Shh! We are passing over the border into Gloucestershire for a few steps – but don't tell the publisher!) Still maintain the heading (right-hand hedge) to another corner gate then continue by the hedge to a gate to a farm drive. Turn right and continue to a lane.

⑥ Turn right to return to Stretton and the Plough.

Maintain the direction through metal barriers. Beyond a metal gate the path is beside the right-hand hedge where rabbits have a township.

A colourful garden in Stretton-on-Fosse

Cherington
The Cherington Arms

| **MAP:** OS LANDRANGER 151 (GR 292369) | **WALK 29** | **DISTANCE:** 4½ MILES |

DIRECTIONS TO START: ABOUT 13 MILES SOUTH OF STRATFORD-UPON-AVON
TURN EASTWARDS OFF THE A3400 ALONG A LANE SIGNED TO CHERINGTON. THE
PUB IS ON THE NORTHERN OUTSKIRTS OF THE VILLAGE NEAR THE RIVER STOUR.
PARKING: THERE IS A LARGE CAR PARK OPPOSITE.

The stroll from Cherington crosses over the infant River Stour near the hollow and ridges marking the site of a large moated mansion. Cherington Mill was grinding corn as late as 1948 and the village church has a tower that has been overlooking the valley since the 15th century.

The route is then to the village of Sutton-under-Brailes. Here is a fine village green where there is the trunk of a huge elm tree (sadly struck down by Dutch elm disease but preserved like a much-loved arthritic granny!). The church here is a gem with much work of the Norman masons to be admired.

The climb up Brailes Hill is a puffing affair – so it should be as this is the second highest peak in the county – but the views make it all worth while. The descent passes a ruined farmstead that is crying out to be rescued although no doubt an electricity supply would cost a lottery fortune.

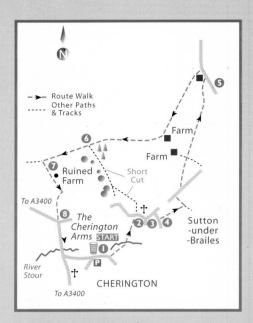

The Cherington Arms

This is an old building stretching back several centuries but it only became a pub after the Second World War. Up to then it was the village shop and indeed the shop front is still in place. Now it is a homely hostelry with a floor friendly to walkers' boots and my Meg even received a warm doggy welcome at the bar. The old orchard is a delight and the river at the bottom of the garden adds to the charm.

The food is simple fare but none the worse for that — just try the home-made Hookie Pie! Hookie is the popular name for the local Hook Norton beer (this is a Hook Norton tenanted house). Vegetarians rave about the couscous with roasted vegetables and children can have half portions of all the dishes. The hours are 6.30 pm to 11 pm on Monday, 12.30 pm to 2.30 pm and 6.30 pm to 11 pm on Tuesday to Saturday and 12 noon to 3 pm and 7 pm to 10.30 pm on Sunday. Telephone: 01608 686233.

The Walk

① Out of the car park turn right. Within 300 yards the road twists sharp right. Keep ahead along a signed path with a large house on the right to a stile leading to a meadow. Bear right to another stile. Pick up the left-hand border of the next field to a bridge and cross the river. Go up the slope. Make for the tower of a church. Climb a stile then another to a lane at Sutton-under-Brailes.

② Turn right to pass the church and the green. (Note: for a shorter walk take the path by the church, joining the route again at point 6 — see sketch map.)

③ By the old elm tree turn right along a lane. Within a few steps take a signed path along a vehicle way by houses on the left.

④ Follow the indicated path through fields then cross a brook. On a farm cart track turn left to a lane. Turn right. Within 200 yards take a signed path on the left. Follow the arrowed way across the open field. Cross the farm drive over stiles. Maintain the heading with stiles to show the way through the fields then aim to the right of a distant bungalow to reach a lane.

⑤ Turn left then left again along a signed bridleway. Climb along a gulley and follow the clear bridleway, passing a farm. Keep ahead along the signed way. We come to a junction of arrowed ways near some fir trees. Keep ahead (fir trees on the left).

pass through but at once turn left to leave the bridleway. The path (number 61a) is beside a left-hand hedge. Go through a corner kissing gate.

⑦ Turn left then right to pass near a ruined farm (keep to the right of this). Go through a gateway just beyond the barns and house then drop downhill away from the house (hedge on the right). Go through a gateway (no gate). Keep ahead along the path numbered 61a. This becomes a cart track which you follow through gates to a road.

⑧ Cross to the opposite lane. Drop down the hill and cross the river. At a junction turn left to the pub.

PLACES OF INTEREST NEARBY

Moreton-in-Marsh is to the south-west of Cherington along country lanes. An important RAF station was located here in the Second World war, now a renowned fire-fighting college. There is an extensive street market every Tuesday. Also in the town is the **Wellington Aviation Museum** which houses an extensive collection of air memorabilia (see Walk 27).

The 'arthritic' elm tree in the village

⑥ Walk at the side of a right-hand hedge to pass through a corner gate. Maintain the heading through another gate. At the next

Whichford
The Norman Knight

MAP: OS LANDRANGER 151 (GR 314347)   **WALK 30**   **DISTANCE:** 3 MILES

DIRECTIONS TO START: ABOUT 15 MILES SOUTH OF STRATFORD-UPON-AVON
TURN EASTWARDS OFF THE A3400 ALONG A LANE SIGNED TO WHICHFORD.
PARKING: THERE IS A CAR PARK IN FRONT OF THE PUB.

The name of the pub gives a clue to the history of the village (which tries hard and almost succeeds to hide itself in beautiful undulating countryside). The knight was from the de Mohun family who came over with William the Conqueror. The lands were included in the Domesday Survey of 1086; and he was probably given the Manor of Whichford as a reward for his services. There is a magnificent village church which has reminders of the de Mohuns and high traceried Perpendicular clerestory windows. We only know there was a castle hereabouts from a mark on the map.

After a stroll through the village, past the old church, there is a sharp climb to the ridge top. Beyond arable lands, the track borders fine woodlands, full of birdlife. The return leg is along a ridge lane.

The Norman Knight

This flower-bedecked free house has been a hostelry for at least a hundred years. In days past the clients would have been the agricultural labourers. Nowadays walkers and tourists join the locals for refreshment and fun – there are pub games like shove halfpenny and Aunt Sally. A Caravan Club site adjoins and there are three self-catering apartments in a charming cottage next to the inn.

The regular beer is Hook Norton Bitter but there is always a guest ale which changes weekly. Being a lover of spicy food I was pleased to see there was a fine assortment of curries, baltis and korma type dishes available. The more traditional snacks are popular with hungry ramblers too. Opening hours are 12 noon to 2.30 pm and 7 pm to 11 pm. Telephone: 01608 684621.

PLACES OF INTEREST NEARBY

Just south of Long Compton (2½ miles from Whichford along lanes) are many historic stones. There are the 60 or so **Rollright Stones** in a circle; more blocks are the **Whispering Knights** solidified by a witch; a few steps away is the 9 ft high **King Stone** (early Bronze Age and perhaps of astronomical significance).

The Walk

① From the car park cross the road and turn right. By the war memorial take the road left.

② Just before the church take a path over a stile on the left. In the pasture follow the right-hand boundary. Turn the corner to the right to another stile. Do not climb this but take a direction over the open field left. Aim for the gate now seen below the ridge. Beyond, climb steeply over a hill pasture to a corner stile on the top of the ridge.

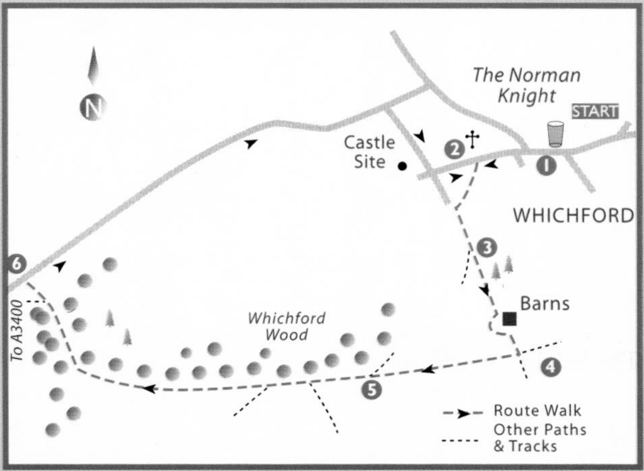

③ Maintain the heading across an arable field, aiming to the right of a row of fir trees. Keep ahead at a waymark post so the old Doctor's Barn is on your left. (Doctor Yeomans was Rector of Whichford at the time of Enclosure in 1806.) At a new barn go left then right along a farm vehicle way. Follow this for 300 yards.

④ At a junction of wide tracks turn right and continue with a hedge on your left. Keep ahead through a far hedge gap and go on to a wood.

The former school house at Whichford

⑤ Follow the edge of the right-hand wood for about ¾ mile. The wide track then enters the wood and you keep ahead to a lane.

⑥ Turn right. The fine upland way drops down after a mile to a junction. Turn right. The lane dips then climbs to the edge of Whichford (the castle site is to the right). Turn left and join the outward route to the Norman Knight.